TOWARDS A PHENOMENOLOGICAL ETHICS

SUNY Series in Contemporary Continental Philosophy
Dennis J. Schmidt, Editor

TOWARDS A PHENOMENOLOGICAL ETHICS

ETHOS AND THE LIFE-WORLD

Werner Marx

With a Foreword by Thomas Nenon

State University of New York Press

Published by
State University of New York Press, Albany

For information, address State University of New York
Press, State University Plaza, Albany, N.Y., 12246

Production by Diane Ganeles
Marketing by Bernadette LaManna

Library of Congress Cataloging-in-Publication Data
Marx, Werner.
    Towards a phenomenological ethics : ethos and the life-world /
Werner Marx.
        p.   cm. — (SUNY series in contemporary continental
philosophy)
    Includes index.
    ISBN 0-7914-0574-5 (alk. paper). — ISBN 0-7914-0575-3 (pbk. :
alk. paper)
    1. Ethics. 2. Phenomenology. I. Title. II. Series.
BJ1031.M316   1992
170—dc20   90-36907
                                                                        CIP

10 9 8 7 6 5 4 3 2 1

Contents

Foreword

I

One way to describe the question that not only motivates and unites the six essays in this book but also permeates all of Werner Marx's philosophical works is: How and where do we find, preserve, perhaps even create measure and order where disorder, chaos, and a ruinous lack of measure threaten to prevail? In our age, an age—as Marx has called it—"between tradition and a new beginning," this question is particularly urgent, for it seems that the traditional guarantors of order, transcendent sources of meaning such as the Greek gods and their secular successors, the forms or the *teloi* inherent in things by nature, as well as the Judeo-Christian God and his secular successor, human reason, are increasingly becoming historical phenomena, at least as far as their ability to serve as universally accepted guideposts for our actions is concerned. They are not gone, their traces still remain efficacious today, and for many persons, in particular the religious, they can be as relevant today as they have ever been. Nonetheless, it can hardly be disputed that they have all ceased to serve as universally recognized and unshakable foundations upon which knowledge and action can be based. Even those who regret this development bear witness to it in their call *back* to the traditional values.

Yet the uniquely modern cultural institution whose task it is to explain things, to discover order and regularity among the things that present themselves to us in the world, that is, science, turns out to be particularly unsuited

1

to the task of explaining things in terms that would not only record and analyze statistically significant patterns but would also provide human beings with a normative standard for their own conduct and address questions of "meaning" and purpose in human life. As Max Weber recognized, modern empirical science can at best help provide an analysis of the effective means to achieve a given end, and it can establish more or less reliable correlations between social background, psychological experiences, and the like, on the one hand, and the probable values and desires of some group or individual, on the other. But it cannot provide a standard, a measure in the classical sense that could serve as a guide for proper conduct in the way that the norms proposed by traditional metaphysical philosophy had purported to be able to do. For not just any order would provide the kind of measure that Marx seeks. Rather, he contends that what is lacking is the kind of measure that had been provided by religion and traditional metaphysics, according to which human beings are endowed with a particular dignity and have responsibilities towards themselves and others. The order of technological efficiency, the simple order of regularities in nature, or even the order that enforces whatever ends a particular individual or group might wish to impose—no matter how "orderly" in the sense of effectiveness this might be—cannot suffice. For what is lacking is a measure, an order that can serve as a guide for the kind of conduct that one has traditionally called "ethical," a measure for distinguishing good from evil in a modern world in which the very meaning of these notions threatens to be lost. This kind of measure is something that modern science or even philosophical counterparts of the scientific approach such as decision theory are unsuited to provide.

Thus what remains is a situation in which it seems that there are no longer any binding guidelines for human action. Each individual must decide for him- or herself what is good and what is evil, what is to be desired, and what must be avoided. And while many may experience this as a positive development, as a liberation from the confines of traditional metaphysics and the moral systems derived from it, major events of our century have also shown that the ends adopted by individuals beyond conventional morality can often be anything but benevolent. For Werner Marx, who was a personal witness to and, along with many close to him, a victim of the catastrophic decline of Germany into a barbarism that prided itself upon its being beyond religious sentimentalities and humanitarianism, the complete loss of order and measure, which had been traditionally supported by principles derived from either the religious or the secular enlightenment versions of the metaphysical tradition, does not present itself as a development that is to be welcomed.

However, even apart from such catastrophic events and the question of whether they must or can be attributed to the decline of the tradition, there is another aspect of modern life that seems to be playing a significant role in Marx's thinking. What replaces the consciousness of human beings as children of God or as rational subjects each endowed with his or her own autonomy and dignity is not always an irrational will-to-power or naked egoism, but more often what Marx refers to as "the everyday indifference" that pervades most of our common lives. What remains is more or less self-concerned individuals caught up in the affairs of daily life, trying to succeed or at least muddle through as best they can within the particular pregiven worlds in which they find themselves. In this day-to-day existence, the prevailing attitude is not necessarily ruthless or brutally callous; rather one is aware of the "other" more as a factor with which one must deal in the course of one's everyday concerns than as someone to be dominated or eliminated. Nonetheless, however, the focus is always upon the way that the other figures into one's *own* affairs and concerns. Furthermore, the question of the nature of one's own existence, the real question of the source of meaning in one's enterprises, is avoided as well. Lacking the norms and standards previously provided by traditional ethics, without the secure sense of a place in the cosmos, the order of creation, or the noumenal realm, modern humanity is faced with a situation in which orientation points threaten to become lost altogether so that life becomes measureless, directionless, at best a search for the satisfaction of individual desires or whims. One perhaps very common way to deal with this situation is not to face it, to immerse oneself so much in one's everyday and individual concerns that one no longer even notes the abyss below and the lack of genuine bonds to those around us. This at least seems to be the danger that Marx perceives and that the six essays in this book are meant to address, each in its own way.

Before looking at each of the essays individually and examining just how each relates to this theme, that is the possibility of finding a way to give a unified meaning to one's life and to overcome the isolation that threatens to predominate our everyday lives in the modern world, I would first like to make a few observations about the method that Marx employs in all of them. These will at the same time serve as a loose commentary on the first essay of the book, which addresses methodological questions concerning the studies which follow.

II

In the Preface to this book, Marx refers to the essays as "phenomenological analyses" that build upon the contributions towards a "nonmetaphysical ethics" that he first began to develop in his important work *Is There A Measure on Earth?*[1] But what do these terms mean here? Given the broad range of thinkers and methods that have claimed the status of phenomenological for themselves, in particular given the differences between the two most important representatives of phenomenology in this century, that is Edmund Husserl and Martin Heidegger, it is important to get clear about just what this notion involves here.

Perhaps more controversially and importantly, what does the term "nonmetaphysical" mean in this context? If, as I contend above, it is the search for order, for a measure that can serve as an orientation for all human beings in our age, that motivates Marx's work, then is it not rather a successor than an alternative to the metaphysical tradition? And if it turns out that the "foundation" upon which the insights of this work are based is the recognition of "mortality" as an inescapable fact about all human beings, something that is part of human nature, then is this not rather a reestablishment of a metaphysical ethics than the overcoming of metaphysics? That in itself would not necessarily have to count as a mark against this enterprise, one should note; it could perhaps serve as an indication that the common dismissal of metaphysics has been too hasty, that it is a mistake to assume that metaphysics has been or should be overcome once and for all. It would nonetheless call into question important aspects of Marx's own interpretation of the analyses presented here. It therefore seems appropriate to examine more closely what it is that makes the studies in this book phenomenological and to what extent and in which sense the outline of an ethics proposed here is significantly different from those presented by traditional metaphysics.

Taken in the broadest sense, phenomenology is simply the attention to "the things themselves," the issues of philosophy, and not to philosophical texts and historical positions and arguments. According to this standard, the method employed in the essays presented in this work is paradigmatically phenomenological. It will of course be apparent to the careful reader just how much here is inspired by Marx's intimate familiarity with important figures and positions from the history of philosophy, in particular those of Aristotle, Hegel, Husserl, and Heidegger; and the extent to which Marx finds himself quite consciously in a critical discussion with other aspects of the tradition, in particular classical liberalism with its emphasis upon rational deliberation and calculation as a guide to choosing the proper action in order to realize one's individual goals and upon the justification of the social dimension of human life strictly in terms of its usefulness for the individual. In spite of this, however, the primary concern of this book is the possibility of a particular kind of life that one might call moral, how it relates to the question of human life in a community, and how it could serve to integrate the life of a person throughout the various spheres in which that person moves. However, mere attention to issues instead of historical positions certainly cannot suffice to characterize the approach involved here as phenomenological, although it is certainly a precondition for the studies to count as such.

What makes these studies phenomenological is the way that they address the issues through an appeal to *experience,* not simply as a report about the author's own individual factual experiences or indeed necessarily about anyone's actual experience, but about the possibility of certain kinds of experiences which any reader should be able to recreate imaginatively on his or her own and thereby see that the possibility for such an experience is universal, even if the reality of it is not. Thus, the method is anything but inductive, since there is no claim about the frequency of the experiences that are analyzed here, nor about a significant statistical correlation between certain kinds of experiences and others which might be expected to follow from them. At the same time, however, it goes beyond conceptual analysis; it is not claimed either that the kinds of connections that are alluded to here are inevitable because logically necessary, or even that these are *the* necessary conditions for the possibility of a moral or an integrated life or of a social consciousness; rather it exhibits possibilities *as* possibilities that any human being could undergo without claiming that in either a logical or an empirical sense they necessarily follow from certain other conditions.

In this regard, the method employed here differs significantly from that of Husserl's phenomenological analyses. Husserl understood phenomenology as an eidetic science that exhibits essential connections, and at least in his middle and later periods saw it as a form of transcendental philosophy that establishes the necessary conditions for the possibility of certain kinds of entities through an analysis of the conditions for the possibility of the genesis of such things within consciousness. In every case, however, his emphasis was upon essential, that is, necessary and invariant structures of various kinds of consciousness and their correlative forms of objects. Marx shares with Husserl the emphasis upon an analysis of things as they actually show themselves to us, that is, to concrete human experience of them, and he shares the conviction with Husserl that the domain of phenomenological analysis is not limited to the experience of any one factual individual; but he departs from Husserl in extending his interest not exclusively or even primarily to necessary connections, but to possibilities as such. His analysis rests neither upon empirical generalizations nor upon conceptual analysis. It is thus still clearly in the phenomenological tradition, however, if he has abandoned the project of exhibiting necessary connections, does this not leave him in a no-man's-land of mere conjecture? If the universal bindingness of its results is lacking, a universal bindingness that one might, in a Husserlian vein, insist is at least part of what constitutes philosophy as a discipline, what is it that makes these analyses "philosophical."

It is important to note that, although Marx is not dealing in experiences that are necessarily shared by everyone, nor even in logically (either in a formal or a transcendental sense) necessary relationships between certain kinds of experiences, he is nonetheless concerned with *structures* of human life and what is involved in them. Although most people may flee their mortality, may ignore the claim to compassion inherent in our implicit awareness of the mortality of the other, in other words even if most people will fail to experience their own nature and the nature of our fellow human beings *as such,* this does not change the fact that mortality is an essential aspect of our own being and the being of all other humans, whether we want to recognize it or not. Therefore, although the claim is not that the experience of mortality as such is universal nor that the experience of it *necessarily* leads one to become a more compassionate person, Marx does suggest that mortality is an essential characteristic of all human beings and that compassion is at least one appropriate response to the recognition of this fact. Furthermore, for anyone who is seeking a way out of the isolation, the meaninglessness, the indifference that seems to predominate in the modern age, this possibility, which is universally present, might be a welcome one. Similarly, in an age in which many are dissatisfied with the idea of community life as a contract, a "deal," or are concerned about the fragmentation of modern life into various seemingly disparate realms with competing or even conflicting priorities and obligations, it does indeed seem helpful to point out basic facts about human existence that can lead to an awareness that would help overcome such individualizing and fragmentating tendencies.

In this respect, Marx's version of phenomenology resembles that of the early Heidegger, for whom the proper subject of phenomenology is that which for the most part does *not* show itself as it is, that which we do not usually experience as such. Heidegger's existential analysis of Dasein concerns the constitution the Dasein and its essential structures, but the truth about the nature of human existence is for Heidegger not something that we are immediately aware of or that we experience directly, but rather a fact that we avoid, that we flee and try actively to forget. In fact, Marx notes that his analysis of the experience of mortality in *Is There a Measure on Earth?* is inspired by Heidegger's analysis of anxiety in *Being and Time.*[2]

Marx departs from Heidegger, however, in the guiding interest, the question that he brings with him from the outset. For Heidegger, the significance of the awareness of death for his project of establishing a fundamental ontology leads him to concentrate upon resoluteness, for in resoluteness a human being faces up to itself as a thrown, projecting out of and into nothingness and thereby becomes capable of seeing the historicality of its own Being and temporality as the backdrop for any understanding of Being. Marx, by contrast, is concerned with the question of whether there is any measure for responsible human conduct, in particular for our dealings with others, in this world. Marx does not deny that the direction of his phenomenological analysis is also determined by a personal existential interest; however, he is convinced that this interest is not merely a personal interest, but a common concern in our age, and that the structures and the possibilities that his analyses reveal are universal structures of human being and possibilities open to anyone who shares these concerns. Thus although personal, the guiding interest is anything but arbitrary, and the structures that are revealed and the possibilities that their recognition open up are supposed to be universal.

If, however, as I suggested at the beginning, this interest is to establish or re-establish some kind of measure, some kind of order in a world that is threatened with the loss of order and measure, isn't this phenomenological project itself just another form of metaphysics? Moreover, if what it is attempting to do is provide a "foundation" for a responsible way of life, an ethos, by searching for universal structures of the human being, is this work not just repeating the gesture of metaphysics that attempts to derive universally valid norms from some notion of human nature? How is this approach different from traditional metaphysical ethics?

Marx's project, it is important to note, is not to destroy (or even deconstruct) or overcome metaphysics. The demise of metaphysics is for him not a goal to be achieved, but rather a fact that one must face. A number of his statements—in particular those on religion and on the Enlightenment's faith in human reason—suggest that, to the contrary, Marx feels if not a kind of nostalgia, then at least a sense of loss at the end of traditional metaphysics. This explains his search for something that could serve to replace it, something that could perform the function that metaphysics traditionally fulfilled without attempting to go back to or restore what is in his view irretrievably lost. In a certain sense, Marx finds himself in a position similar to that of many Enlightenment figures, including Immanuel Kant. They saw their efforts as an attempt to replace religion and dogmatic metaphysics with a new account of the regularities in nature and a new moral code founded

upon a secular, critical analysis of this world and the role of
human reason within it, both of which would retain what
had been correct and valuable in previous metaphysical
systems, but provide it with a more appropriate foundation
based not upon other-worldly entities, but upon natural objects and natural human faculties and needs.

That an ethics for our age cannot go back to a metaphysics based upon the existence of other-worldly entities,
upon a transcendent God that will serve as the source for
measure today, but rather than any measure in our age
must be sought here on earth is a recurrent theme of
Marx's previous publication, *Is There a Measure on Earth?*
The impossibility of such a return is less the theme than
the starting point of this book. More relevant is the question whether or not the traditional alternative to transcendent, nonnatural sources of measure cannot be provided by
the faculty of human reason, a kind of second, higher nature, than can serve as the norm for human conduct and at
the same time also be the source of a change in human behavior from an unreflected, indifferent existence or a self-
centered egoism to a more responsible and virtuous life.
Here too, however, the impossibility of going back to the
traditional secular metaphysics, in which the foundation
for ethics is sought in the rationality of human life—either
as a fact or more often as a normative demand—is more
assumed than argued, more taken as the starting point
than the theme of his study. Marx does not fail to note,
however, that to a large degree even the modern notion of
rationality has been perverted from the Kantian idea of
pure practical reason as respect for the moral law into
mere purposive rationality, that is, deliberations and cal-
culations concerning the most efficient means to attain a
given end. Such "rationality" in Marx's view certainly cannot provide the kind of orientation he is seeking. But since
in a predominantly secular age, this is—or rather has ap-
peared to be—the only possibility remaining after the decline of religious faith as a universally recognized basis for
ethics, the position outlined by Marx is consciously developed in contradistinction to ethical systems in the modern

tradition. When Marx describes the ethics he proposes as "nonmetaphysical," this is what he has in mind. What he means is that the kind of transformation of one's life that he is describing does not depend upon an appeal to reason, does not require deliberation, decision, and a separate act of will that would implement the suggestion advanced by practical reason (in the case of various utilitarian systems) or that it involves an autonomous demand by one's own consciousness of the necessity to act only in accordance with those rules to which one could assent as an impartial rational spectator (the Kantian view). Marx's position, as developed both in his earlier work *Is There a Measure on Earth?* and in this work, is not presented as a study of the possibility of an ethical system based upon rational principles, but as an indication of the possibilities for a change in one's life that can be brought about by a specific experience, that is, the experience of one's own mortality. Such a change in one's attitude toward one's own life and towards others would not require the kind of deliberation or appeal to universally valid rules that characterizes most recent ethical systems. The position sketched out in this work emphasizes the importance of attunements, basic attitudes from which particular kinds of actions follow more or less automatically so that it is not necessary to postulate a further faculty, namely will, to implement what one rationally recognizes to be (either in a strictly moral or in a utilitarian sense) the right thing to do.

The term "nonmetaphysical" in the present context signifies that the change in one's conduct, one's ethos that is described here (a) does not have a theological foundation (even though the kinds of virtues that are commensurate with it are closely related to those of the Judeo-Christian tradition); and (b) that it is not derived from or dependent upon a system of rational principles that can serve as normative rules for human action. Accordingly, the issues that figure prominently in traditional ethical treatises, for example, the role of deliberation, decision-making, casuistics, metaethical justification and the like, are for the most part missing here.

To some extent the prominence of the term "nonmeta-physical" here is still a result of the way the basic insights that guide this work were reached in Marx's previous work. *Is There a Measure on Earth?* was explicitly characterized by its author as an attempt to "think Heidegger further," to make use of Heideggerian insights and themes in ways that Heidegger himself had failed to do in order to answer questions that Marx recognized as his own and not Heidegger's. In fact, Marx begins that work by showing how the question concerning a measure for good and evil in the realm of human action has no real place, how it gets lost in Heidegger's thinking from his early work *Being and Time* up through his middle and very latest essays. The determinations that Marx employs in establishing what he calls "foundations for a nonmetaphysical ethics" are nonetheless borrowed from Heidegger. Central among them are the notions of *Gestimmtheit* or emotional attunement as the dimension that determines not only a person's perspective upon herself and the things and persons around her but also gives rise to commensurate attitudes and actions; and *Angst,* specifically *Angst* in the face of one's own mortality, as an unsettling experience that is capable of transforming one's attitude of everyday indifference or even individualistic egoism into a caring, compassionate attitude toward one's fellow human beings. A closer description of the results of that book and its relationship to the essays contained in this work will be provided below. For the present question concerning the status of these essays as "nonmetaphysical," what is important to note is that Marx follows Heidegger in avoiding the construction of a "subject" as an agent whose actions follow from rational deliberation and that the "foundation" that he identifies is not a set of rules or principles, neither a justification of certain rights or a deduction of any particular duties, but rather a description of kinds of experiences that can lead to a new attitude about and conduct toward others.

Marx does not deny, indeed he even affirms that the kind of measures he seeks share a great deal with traditional metaphysical measures. Not only does their content coincide with the traditional virtues, but their form has much in common with the way that metaphysical standards were viewed as well. They should have a certain binding character, they should be applicable throughout various situations ("self-same" in Marx's words), and in this sense they should be "manifest" or "univocal."[3] In section 4 of the second essay in the present collection, he even refers to them as measures that are not only binding but also are absolute and certain. They differ from metaphysically conceived measures in that they are no longer supposed to stand over against the persons for whom they are relevant as something "transcendent," but rather be immanent to the kinds of life that these persons lead, that is, they are to be measures "in which one dwells."[4] Nonetheless they do possess a substantiality that guarantees that their binding character extends beyond the purely subjective realm. For this reason also, the metaphysically so significant term "foundation" seems applicable here. The kind of emotional transformation Marx describes is not only a "foundation" in the sense that it can underlay a basic change in all of one's particular views and actions, but also in the sense that it possesses the certainty, the stability, and at least potential universalizability that recall the specific connotations of traditional notion of "foundation" as well. When Werner Marx asks, "Is a Nonmetaphysical Ethics Possible?" his question therefore does not imply that an ethics for our age may not and should not have anything in common with traditional ethical systems from the history of metaphysics, but rather that it cannot rely upon certain traditional metaphysical assumptions, for example, the existence of the realm of the divine as a measure for man or the assumption of the basic rationality of humanity, as its basis. The question Marx asks can be restated rather simply in the following way: "Is an ethics possible today that does not depend upon either transcendent beings or upon an appeal to human rationality?"

The reader would thus do well not to become too caught up in the characterization of the studies here as "nonmetaphysical," since their purpose is after all not to provide a theoretical treatise about the possibilities and limitations of metaphysics in the practical sphere today, but rather to show the possibility of a kind of experience that can change our way of looking at ourselves and others. As such, the most important question is whether the experiences to which Marx is pointing here are genuine possibilities for us today and whether they can and do lead to the kinds of transformations he indicates. The answer to this question is completely independent of the question whether or not and in which sense the description of them in this work is metaphysical or not. This is perhaps an important point to make in view of current talk, as vague as it is pervasive, about the end of metaphysics and philosophy today as "postmetaphysical." In this situation, Marx's approach can serve to remind us that, even under the assumption that we are indeed at the end of the metaphysical tradition, one task for philosophy is not only to discuss the history of metaphysics, its limitations, and the reasons for its demise but also to inquire what possibilities for thought still present themselves to us concerning the pressing practical concerns which confront us in our age. He maintains that with the collapse of traditional metaphysical systems, the foundation for responsible conduct, the basis for a respect for ourselves and others as human beings, has been lost as well. His aim is to try to point out some simple facts that could help fill the vacuum that this loss has created.

In what follows then, I would like to address at least briefly the major theses of the essays contained in this volume, with special attention to the second essay because of the pivotal role the insights developed there play in all of the others.

III

A comparison between the introductory essay to Marx's previous work, an essay also bearing the title "Is There a Measure on Earth?," and the second essay in the present volume reveals a clear continuity in the basic theme and

yet a striking difference in approach. In both studies, the
central claim is that an experience of one's own mortality
can lead to a change in one's attitude and conduct towards
other persons so that one becomes a more compassionate, a
charitable human being willing to recognize the humanity
of others as well. Whereas in the former work, however,
Marx develops his position through a discussion of the de-
ficiencies and untapped potential of Heidegger's thought,
"Ethos and Mortality" has the character of a more or less
straightforward phenomenological analysis of the kinds of
experiences that can lead to such a transformation and the
nature of the attitudes that can result from it. Although
Marx still continues to borrow heavily from the Heideggerian analyses of phenomena such as *Gestimmtheit* (attunedness) and *Befindlichkeit* (situatedness), *Angst,* and
death, the emphasis is less upon what Heidegger did or did
not do with these determinations, but rather what genuine
phenomenological insights are contained in them that can
be relevant for the kind of transformation of character that
Marx has in mind here. Other major differences are a re-
estimation of the role of rational insight in the essay in this
volume and the inclusion of a analysis of the possible effects
of a person's transformed way of relating to other persons
upon those persons themselves.

In both essays, the crucial role of *Gestimmtheiten,*
emotional predispositions, in determining one's actions is
emphasized as an alternative to calculative rule-governed
ethical systems. The *Is There a Measure on Earth?* book
even gives the impression that rationality simply is calculative deliberation, or at best a reflective consciousness of
the universalization of rules and maxims. Emotions appear
to be something that, if not necessarily opposed to, are then
at least independent of reason. One of the most interesting
changes between the two works is the fact that in this
work, one finds the statement "one's emotional attunement" often complemented by the phrase "and rational insight." Marx recognizes that reflection on rules and
conscious deliberation are not the only forms of rationality
that the tradition espoused, that Aristotle, for example,

had discerned a kind of rational perception, an immediate recognition of what is right and wrong, what is demanded in a situation, and that this kind of rational insight was not opposed to, but rather goes hand in hand with a corresponding kind of emotional attunement. In the case of the virtuous person, for example, one is predisposed to do what one recognizes is right: to ask whether one knows what is right or whether one simply feels it is misleading in the majority of cases. Rather, what happens in the case of the truly virtuous person is that one finds oneself inclined to do what one sees as the right thing to do. To put it in terms of the current discussion in America on expert knowledge, what Marx seems to be pointing out is simply that the expert in the realm of practical conduct will simply do what he or she recognizes is the right thing to do without necessarily having recourse to rules that could be articulated or to any kind of conscious deliberations. If by "rational," one means conscious deliberation or the subordination of one's conduct under rules, then this kind of *ethos* will be outside the realm of the rational; if one takes the rational to include immediate practical insights into what a particular situation demands, then one's reaction—as long as it corresponds to what is appropriate in the given situation—is indeed rational. In his explicit recognition that such prereflective recognition of the practical right does play an important role in the development and stabilization of a moral character, Marx's perspective on the tradition shifts as well. Whereas in the former book, Marx emphasizes the extent to which his outline of a foundation for an ethics for our age differs from traditional ethical proposals, we see him here showing how the kind of experiences he is pointing to are closely related to the phenomena referred to by such traditional figures as Aristotle and Hegel. In a certain sense, without de-emphasizing what is novel in his own position, Marx now enlists elements from the history of philosophy as allies against a specifically modern tendency to reduce reason to calculative rationality. Thus, his approach is in some respects an alternative to traditional systems, but in many respects can be seen as an extension that builds upon the insights of other ethical theorists, and in some respects even a defense of important traditional insights against contemporary interpretations that would falsify them.

The other major difference, the addition of an analysis of the possible effects of a compassionate bearing towards others upon the other person, is contained in section 3 of the essay "Ethos and Mortality." It is important to see that here, too, Marx's points to a possibility of human community that is not based on negotiation, on contracts or rights of individuals, but on a spontaneous recognition of the needs of others that moves one to feel a bond with the other and out of that bond to recognize the other as a fellow mortal and behave accordingly. The other, who experiences the compassion, the recognition that results from this attitude can realize that this opens up a new dimension of human interaction, one that is not based on negotiation, or contract.

Through his use of the symbols "A" and "B," Marx's presentation of the possibilities of human experience that are at issue here seems distant, abstract, almost detached. This appearance is, I think, deceiving. The distance here is not the distance of detachment, but rather the distance of reverence in the face of that which is most sacred within the realm of human relations, that spontaneous recognition of the other in his or her uniqueness, need, and dignity, not as a law-giver or an owner of rights that I *must* grant him or her, but as a fellow human who as a mortal, is not just a representative of the human condition of mortality in general, but has his or her own particular needs, problems, and ways of coping with life that deserve my compassion and recognition. Perhaps only the poet has words for the sacredness of the moment in which the indifference of everyday life and the isolation of individuals is bridged and human beings come together in mutual compassion and understanding. This is the moment that I think Marx is trying to describe here.

Less markedly so, but with the same basic reserve, Marx describes in the second essay in this book and in his previous work the experience that is at the heart of his phenomenological analyses of a possibility for transformation of the common *ethos* in our age: the experience of one's mortality. Here is where the realms of philosophy and poetry intersect in the articulation of possibilities of human experience that are universal, but for the most part lay hidden. Marx remains philosopher here, he seeks to articulate the experience in *Bestimmungen* or determinations, and leaves the more graphic description to other kinds of writers; however, for the empathetic reader, what he is trying to bring out is clear. He describes this experience as *entsetzende Angst* in the face of the constant invention of human mortality, death, into our lives.

The word *Entsetzen* is common in German and expresses a sense of shock, being horrified. This is part of what Marx means, but he also goes back to the root meaning of *Ent-setzen*, throwing someone into a different state, literally dis-placing or setting them into a different mode than the normal one. Marx contends that the power of the experience of mortality consists in just this ability that it has to thrust one out of the normal parameters of everyday life and confront one with the deepest and most unsettling truths about ourselves, the truth that, to use Marx's words, "we are constantly and every moment dying." Death here, following Heidegger, is seen not as a singular event that occurs at the end of our lives, but as the finitude, the nihilating nothingness that permeates the very core of our lives. Marx is sparse in his description of the ways that this, our mortality, touches us, but from the descriptions provided by Heidegger in sections 48–52 of *Being and Time* and Marx's previous hints about how it effects us in *Is There a Measure on Earth?*,[5] we learn it thrusts each of us back upon ourselves and isolates us; that it makes us come face to face with the precariousness and perishability of all our projects and achievements; that it leaves us with a feeling of helplessness; and that it makes us realize that the seeming objectivity of meaning is mere illusion, the seeming endless multitude of possibilities open to us is continually becoming more and more restricted as the present constantly becomes an irretrievable past, and that we are radically dependent upon things other than ourselves to realize even the few limited possibilities available to us.

In the face of this inescapable fact, the solution or at least the proper response, Marx proposes, is not Heideggerian resoluteness, but rather the realization that one is not alone in this plight, but rather finds oneself faced with a truth about human being as a whole, a truth about every person as an individual. The realization makes it possible for an experience that initially isolates us to become one that subsequently leads us to other human beings, that expands our sphere of concern beyond ourselves and our own projects and problems to the other, who has become our salvation in an hour of need.

Most of Marx's analysis speaks clearly for itself. One further point does deserve to be noted; however, namely, the fact that precisely because the realization of one's mortality is a radically individuating experience, the compassion that grows out of it is directed to the other as a unique individual in his or her mortality as well. The paradoxical truth is that mortality as a universal structure of human life is at the same time in each case *my own,* or for the compassionate person *your own* as well. The solidarity that emerges is then directed not to the abstract human community, to all others as copies of me, but is rather a relationship to each individual other as individual, as "other" not just as the same or different from me, but as someone with his or her own unique concerns, projects, and problems. The *otherness* of the other is respected even though the "other" is no longer indifferent or alien to me.

IV

Once one has understood the possibility of a transformation in one's *ethos* that Marx unfolds in the essay "Ethos and Mortality," the fundamental message of the subsequent essays becomes clear as well. Genuine meaning in one's own life and genuine community are possible once one has come to face one's mortality and to recognize other persons as the only salvation from the indifference of everyday life and the isolation of mortality confronted alone.

Marx begins the study on "Ethos and Sociality" with the remark that his use of the term "person" will be much stricter than the normal usage of the word in English (which is also the way it has used these introductory remarks). To call someone a "person" as opposed to an "individual" is to refer to his or her essential relationship to a community and society. The particular theme of the essay is the question: How this essential structure of human beings, their personhood or sociality, can become a genuine and meaningful part of their lives either by being raised out of the everyday indifference, or by transforming the preestablished and therefore almost mindless relationships to other persons around us into sincere concerns. It turns out that here, too, the experience of one's own mortality and the transformed attitude and conduct towards others that can result from it can elevate sociality from a fact about one's existence that one hardly recognizes to an important aspect of one's daily life, so that one becomes a more compassionate and just member of the society in which one lives.

What must be avoided, and what this experience can help one overcome, is the traditional metaphysical opposition between the sphere of subjectivity on the one hand, and objectivity on the other; or the opposition between subjects as self-enclosed agents each striving to maximize their ends over against those of others with whom they find themselves confronted. Here, too, Marx recognizes that he is not in complete opposition to previous philosophers. Husserl's determination of the life-world as a sphere in which we live or "dwell," not as subjects but as members, can help avoid the subject/object dichotomy. Hegel's notion of "ethical life" (*Sittlichkeit*) provides an alternative to the contract model of society. But Marx's unique contribution is his emphasis on the role of emotions in social life. The importance of becoming more conscious, better aware of what is for the most part ignored in our lives is a common theme throughout the history of philosophy. In Marx's sketch of social life, however, this is not so much a matter of intellect as of prepredicative attitudes that issue more or less automatically in socially responsible conduct; nor is it, by contrast to Hegel, a matter of laws and rules as much as it is of voluntary and spontaneous actions.

Marx admits that an established order, a constitution, is indeed necessary for social life in a larger community or state, but even here the aim is to establish a legal order that allows for and is complemented by compassionate behavior between the persons who constitute a society and thereby truly render it a community.

In the subsequent essays, the question of order is reintroduced as the question concerning the order of the world. The study entitled "Is There One World?" sets the stage for the final three essays, all of which are devoted to the theme of the unity and meaning of "the world." With the introduction of the theme "world," it might, at first glance, appear that a radical shift in the theme of the book occurs. For typically one might assume that, at least in the absence of a divine principle as the metaphysical source of everything that exists and the guarantor of order in the cosmos, the question of the meaning of the universe and the practical question concerning the meaning of life are quite distinct. As it turns out, however, and as these essays demonstrate, the two questions turn out to be basically one—at least in their modern versions. For, although at the beginning of the metaphysical tradition, that is, for the Greeks and the medievals, the question of the meaning of the world was presented as an inquiry into the meaning of the cosmos and in particular the ultimate principle behind it, for example, *logos* or the Christian God; in the modern age the unity of the world, if there is to be any unity at all, comes to be considered as the result of the ordering principle of subjectivity. The world becomes increasingly viewed as the correlate of the human activity of knowing so that the question concerning the unity and meaning of the world becomes equivalent to the question concerning the unity of subjective consciousness, the underlying structure of which is temporality.

Marx reviews the developments in the history of philosophy which call into question the assumption that consciousness itself is a unity or a complete whole in the way that traditional metaphysics had assumed. The question of the world now shifts from the question of the unity of the cosmos to the unity of consciousness, and it becomes clear that if there is any unity at all, it is at best a formal unity. An examination of the lives of individuals shows that in fact we do not live in one world, but in a plurality of worlds. Once the notion of world has shifted from an emphasis upon nature or the cosmos to the life-worlds in which we as human beings are constantly engaged, it becomes clear that the traditional metaphysical assumption that the world must be either a seamless unity or an integrated whole is highly questionable. Is it not the case, Marx asks, that we all are capable of living in a number of worlds, many of which are hardly compatible with one another? Moreover, if we no longer assume that there is some one external principle uniting them all, then can one not inquire whether there is anything at all that unites them other than the fact that they are in some way or another *mine?* For many, religion has traditionally provided the one all-encompassing framework out of which each of the particular spheres in which we live our lives have been interpreted and evaluated. For those for whom religion no longer fulfills this function, Marx asks whether there is anything else that could serve to integrate the diverse worlds in which we all live?

If there is such an integrative power, then it would have to be a unifying and underlying meaning throughout our practical lives he concludes in the essay "The Life-Worlds in Their Multiplicity." It thus turns out that, taken in this sense, the question concerning the meaning of the world(s) and the meaning of our practical lives coincide. As Marx points out in section 5 of that essay, however, one essential feature of our everyday worlds is the fact that the question of meaning as such does not normally emerge in them. Each world in which we live has the character of something that is quasi-objective, it appears as something stable, pregiven, and substantial. If there is something that unites them or underlies them all, it would have to come from a source outside our everyday worlds, something that emerges when we somehow suspend them and move outside of them. Such an integrative force would have to be able to permeate all of these worlds, but not be restricted to any one of them. Marx maintains that attitudes and moods have such a permeating power that, when they are ethical attitudes, can be comprehensive and extend into all particular worlds. If there is such an integrative force then, it would have to consist in an ethical attitude; the power of compassion as developed in the study on "Ethos and Mortality" is just such an ethical attitude that is possible in our world today. Thus, the study of worlds and the possibility of their integration today culminates in the suggestion that the experience of mortality and the resulting ethical attitude of compassion toward others is a viable possibility for integrating the many worlds in which all of us live today thus giving them a unified meaning. These essays, rich in phenomenological insight into the nature of life-worlds and the problems which we face in moving from one to another, are worthwhile just on this account alone; but taken together with the essays at the beginning of this book, they present powerful testimony to the way that the experience of mortality to which Werner Marx points can help to provide the measure and order that—not only in Marx's view—are so lacking in our world today.

—Thomas Nenon

Preface

The present book continues the train of thought inaugurated in my *Is There a Measure on Earth?* (Chicago UP, 1987). In that work, I proceeded from the *nonmetaphysical fundamental determinations* with which Martin Heidegger thought counter to the philosophical tradition. In contrast to that tradition, he no longer defined the essence of human being as the *animal rationale* and the *sujectum* endowed with reason. Admittedly, against Heidegger's intentions, who did not unfold the possibility of a nonmetaphysical ethics, I attempted to disclose and think through the matters at the basis of these fundamental determinations with respect to further possibilities enclosed in them. The most important result turned out to be that for those humans who have experienced their mortality, a measure for responsible action may become effective.

The contributions of the present book are joined to this result. The phenomenological analyses of the transformative path on which the measure of the capacity for compassion can be revealed, is substantially expanded; they are complemented by inquiries into social ethics and reflections towards a nonmetaphysical ethics in general. In the second part of the book, we undertake the attempt to relate the ethical force of com-passion to the "objective" side of our existence, to the fact; namely, that we always already live in many worlds and in many contexts of meaning, and that precisely this constitutes the fundamental trait of our being in the life-world.

The contributions of this book make up separate studies complete in themselves. Still, our effort to provide fun-

25

damental determinations for a nonmetaphysical ethics can only be executed in retrospect by a passage through all the contributions. The individual studies, however, can only demonstrate central ways of access to a nonmetaphysical ethics that has not yet been written as such. Hence, they do not want to be merely acknowledged as fully developed results.

I would like to thank Hans Rainer Sepp, who has supported me in the preparation of this publication.

—Werner Marx

A Note on the Translation

Werner Marx frequently uses new and compound words whenever the occasion calls for it. In general, we have tried to harmonize the translation of these with Thomas Nenon's and Reginald Lilly's translation of Marx's previous book, *Is There a Measure on Earth?* (Chicago UP, 1987). Marx usually explains these words as he introduces them in their particular meaning, so that no lengthy commentary is required here. Still, since most of these words are particularly resistant to English, we offer the following account of our choices.

Two terms will be familiar to those conversant with Heidegger's philosophy. *Gestimmtheit,* which refers to the phenomenon that one is always in a particular mood, has been rendered as *attunement.* Marx always uses the word in this formal sense, and whenever he refers to one particular content of this attunement, he writes *Stimmung,* which we translate with the customary *mood.* A corollary of attunement is *Befindlichkeit,* which ordinarily has a psychological meaning (the way one feels; *sich wohl befinded* means to feel fine) as well as the spatial one of being located in a particular place (thus, the Capitol *befindet sich,* is located in Washington, D.C.). Playing on these meanings and taking our cue from the fact that, in English, one can be *in*disposed, we translate it as *disposition* (and here we differ from Nenon and Lilly, who opted for the more customary "state of mind"). Marx's own understanding of both words can be found on p. 44 [in the manuscript].

The most recalcitrant words are those related to nearness. *Der Nächste,* literally the one who is nearest or closest

27

to me, is known as the *neighbor* whom the Bible enjoins us to treat with neighborly love. Following the example of neighborly love (*Nächstenliebe*), Marx coins the word *Nächstenethik,* which we translate as *ethics of neighborliness.* The *Nächste* who is the subject of this ethics, we translate as *neighbor,* occasionally adding to it "as one who is near," depending on the context. Another one who is near is the *Mitmensch:* the human being who is there with us and who partakes of the same humanity. Sadly, since there is neither an English word for *mensch* nor the possibility of using *with* in a compound word in this sense, we have been forced to settle for the customary *fellow-man.* We will return below to the sexism implicit in those three letters.

German has many words that denote a relation of some kind, whereas English has only one. One that Marx frequently uses, and which is indeed at the very core of this book, is *verhalten,* both as a verb and as a noun, and the noun *Verhältnis* derived from it. *Sich verhalten zu,* which can be used for human beings and things alike, means to stand in a certain relation to someone or something, with the implication that this relation determines one's attitude or comportment towards that to which one is thus related. Depending on the emphasis in each case, we have translated it as *comportment towards, relation to, how one relates to* (one's world, one's neighbor, etc.). It should be borne in mind that whenever the words *relation* or *relate* appear in this book, it is never intended in an abstract or formal sense. Relations also pervade the word *Zusammenhang,* connection, and *Sinnzusammenhang.* Marx uses the latter to denote the plurality of meaning, the fact that no single meaning exists in isolation but is connected in relations of reciprocal determination with a host of other meanings. Precisely in order to emphasize this latter character, we have translated it as *context of meaning.*

Sinn is translated throughout as *meaning.* Marx uses it in a particular way when he coins the verb *sinnverstehen* and *sinnerfahren,* the understanding of meaning and the experience of meaning. Meaning here is not simply any meaning in a formal semantic sense, but meaning in its manifold connections mentioned above. The compounds are used to indicate that understanding and experience are not empty epistemological categories, but meaningful relations (in the sense of *Verhalten*). Thus he often speaks of *das sinn-verstehende Leben,* life not as a biological or anthropological phenomenon, but as the fundamental mode of human being oriented towards meaning. To translate the adjectival forms of these verbs, we have had recourse either to the gerund (*comportment understanding meaning* for *das sinn-verstehende Verhalten,* for example) or to a relative clause (*the life that experiences meaning* for *das sinnerfahrende Leben*). Neither of these solutions is particularly graceful, but given the fact that these compounds usually occur in long sentences, we decided not to add to their length even more by a substantial paraphrase.

Though it is grammatically masculine in German, the word *Mensch* does not refer exclusively to the male portion of the human species. The usual makeshifts "person" and "individual" were unavailable in this case, since Marx uses both words in a special terminological sense. While we have tried to substitute *one* and *one's* whenever possible, the threat of ungainly syntactic complications has regrettably prevented us from eliminating every instance of *man, he* and *his*. Whereas *Mensch* is syntactically, though not semantically, masculine, the German *Person* is feminine, and we have availed ourselves of this fact to provide something of an antidote to the implicit bias in the "generically" used *man.* Thus we have adopted the feminine pronouns *she* and *her* for *person.* This is not to be construed as meaning that Marx was thinking only of women whenever he wrote "person," and consequently that only women are social beings. Rather, it is intended to impart to the male reader something of the experience women go through by being constantly bombarded with this obnoxious "generic" *man*— and what could be more apposite in a book whose focus is the "transformative experience"?

—Stefaan Heyvaert

CHAPTER 1

Is a Non-Metaphysical Ethics Possible?

I

In my publications, I have suggested that the historical situation of the philosophers of today is characterized by the fact that they are "condemned" to think in a space between "tradition" and "another beginning." Perhaps a reflection on this domain of movement of our present philosophical endeavors may inaugurate a meditation on the possibility of a "non-metaphysical" ethics. Our eyes should be above all on the method and the object of a non-metaphysical ethics.

Let us recall the two sides that delimit the space within which we must engage in philosophy today. One of them is formed by our tradition, broadly speaking the epoch of "metaphysics." Here, one does not need to share Martin Heidegger's view, according to which "Metaphysics," beginning already with Socrates, Plato, and Aristotle, has been expressed in all the configurations of Western culture. The basic features characteristic of this ensemble, cited not only by Heidegger but many others as well include its ontological and theological constitution, and the determinative nature of reason conceived as light, which actually or potentially assured the rationality of reality. Thus, at the end of this epoch, Hegel stated the then still valid conviction that "reason rules the world." Further features of this epoch are the determination of being as substance in its different varieties—conceiving, again with Hegel, substance also as subject—along with the determination of freedom as the utmost manifestation of the subjectivity of the subject. To these basic features we must add that already Aristotle had thought man as a *zoon logon echon* and a *zoon politikon*. This one side, delimiting the interspace of our philosophical endeavor today, continues to rule even though it is often only in the ruin-like form co-determined by those developments that have dissolved the tradition. We shall just hint at these with the names of Nietzsche, Marx, and Freud.

The *other* side delimiting this space would be that of "another beginning," already forethought by "another thinking" in different projects but never become a reality— "another beginning" with an eye to a total conception of reality as such and of human reality in particular.

The space in which we philosophize our philosophical thought takes place today—be it by working on the tradition historically in manifold different attempts, or by merely repeating it under other names, or by exploring completely different methods, like analytic thought or a thinking oriented towards the structure of language forms—has known the endeavors of "another" thinking, like that of Rosenzweig, Buber, Ebner, Maritain, Marcel, Levinas, and Heidegger, although their projects have as yet brought forth no "other" kind of Being. My own works also attempt to think against metaphysics in order, in this sense of the "non" in the expression "non-metaphysical," to disassociate myself from metaphysical determinations. Thus I designate my attempt at an ethics as a *non*-metaphysical one. I suppose that I have not succeeded completely in disassociating my thought radically from metaphysics because many metaphysical determinations are already sedimented implicitly in our language. Precisely this characterizes philosophical thought within the space between tradition and "another beginning."

My view is that it is not possible for us, finding ourselves thinking philosophically between tradition and another beginning, to already develop an ethics in the sense of a fully matured set of basic determinations. Nor is it necessary to share Heidegger's view that only the "disciplines" outlined by Plato and Aristotle may bear this name. One can speak of an "ethics" without meaning a fully elaborated project. Yet one can also forgo the name ethics and be content to speak of "descriptions of *ethos*," as is the case in the contributions contained in this book.

We find the appropriate method of describing an *ethos* within the realm of non-metaphysical thought in a *phenomenological* explication. This is because phenomenology, as we understand it, is able to interpret that which reveals itself, to describe in a retracing by experience and thought that which, emerging from concealment, becomes manifest as given in itself—that which appears in this way, the phenomenon. Phenomenology interprets without referring to psychological or other theories, for it brings the respective matter at issue into view in order to clarify the structural features and relations of meaning that lie within it, to uncover them insofar as they were hidden, and to bring them into the "open."

The following descriptions of our *ethos* in our life-world do not provide mere depictions of actual, contemporary events. For phenomenology may not simply "depict" what is experienced in each respective case. It rather attempts to interpret a structural whole in such a way that it does not grasp an individual entity, but the *being* of this entity. When, in the following, we seek to understand how an individual, based on the experience of his or her own mortality and sociality, can set off on a path that transforms his or her whole character, it cannot be a question of describing this path as a factual one. Disregarding the sphere of actual occurrences, phenomenology must rather point out the possibility of such a path of transformation solely from the *structures of human Being* and the world.

In addition, we must realize that the phenomenon of a path of transformation that proceeds from the experience of one's own mortality and sociality, does not constitute the phenomenon of something "real" but of something "possible." And a phenomenological description can indeed be applied to this. Admittedly, we must then designate the possibility whose interpretation is at issue beforehand in order to be able to describe it as *accurately* as possible. The possibility with which we are concerned can be formulated in the question: How can a person, on the basis of a preceding experience of his own mortality and sociality be brought to the greatest possible appropriation of responsibility and ultimately to the virtue of com-passion? It is not the object of our investigation to describe the possible paths leading to contrary attitudes that can indeed also be *results* of that initial experience, like closing oneself off with regard to others and the world at large. Each of these requires rather an analysis of its own.

We can repudiate the suspicion that we have resorted to arbitrary constructions by focusing our inquiry on the said possibility of a path of transformation, by the method of phenomenological explanation we employ for this inquiry, and by our intention to orient ourselves solely to those states of affairs which can be shown to spring from the being of man at each of the individual "stations" of the transformatory path.

II

What is, more specifically, the theme and the aim of the following descriptions? It will be a matter of rendering visible that, and how, transformations within the element of the emotions are possible—transformation precipitated by a radical change in attunement that can liberate man from the imprisonment constituted by the *indifference* towards his fellow-man and the community.

Metaphysics, particularly since Aristotelian teleology, has attributed a far greater role to rationality than to emotionality when treating questions of morality and ethical conduct. Admittedly Spinoza (in his *Ethica ordine geometrico demonstrata* despite its rationalistic method), Pascal, and later Schopenhauer, Kierkegaard, and others saw clearly the importance of emotionality for the ethical consciousness. Hume, in particular, described emotionality in thorough-going observations in his *Enquiry into the Principals of Morals*. However, it was above all Husserl who put great importance on the role of feeling in the constitution of a "pure" ethics in his numerous lectures on ethics. Husserl did not, however, discuss the role of emotionality in the formation of virtues, rather he outlined an "ethics of value" as had already been carried out by Max Scheler—though on the basis of Husserl's insights—in particular in his *Formalism in Ethics and the Material Ethics of Value.*

At any rate, our real adversary is not Aristotelian teleological rationality but rather the one described by Alisdair MacIntyre as Weberian "purposive rationality" in his book *After Virtue* (London 1974). Under this title, MacIntyre subsumes not only the determining influence of the whole period of the Enlightenment (in particular Kant's doctrine of the categorical imperative for the autonomous moral subject) but also the whole utilitarian movement, Marxism, and Neo-Marxism. For he claims that they all share the view that the "highest concept" for "the moral life is the concept of a 'rule'" (MacIntyre p. 112). He further points out that this purposive rationality has only been countered by Nietzsche's conviction that traditional philosophy never justified these universally valid rules of rationality and that, apart from this, it obscured the fundamentally irrational phenomenon of the will. MacIntyre's thesis hold that in this conflict between Weberian "purposive rationality" and Nietzsche's "irrationality" there is no universally shared conception of what constitutes the "good" for a community. He sees the only possible solution to this conflict in a rehabilitation of Aristotelian philosophy and its teleological rationality, since it leads to the formation of virtues. MacIntyre regards the main task of a contemporary philosophical ethics as being concerned with the *quality of character* and not in the following of rules. One can agree with MacIntyre on this and one should join him in seeking a possibility to fend off a Nietzschean rejection of all morality and ethical norms, which is indeed not nonmetaphysical but anti-metaphysical.

We cannot, however, agree with MacIntyre's contention that Aristotelean teleology is the only possibility of rehabilitating a doctrine of virtues. Such a doctrine is certainly needed in order to understand at all the function and authority of rules. However, this is not afforded by most contemporary cognitivist ethics, like constructivist ethics, the attempts at rational reconstruction of the Kantian and Hegelian ethics of consciousness, the Marxist and Neo-Aristotelian ethics, the structuralist and analytically orientated ethics, and Karl Otto Apel's transcendental-pragmatic ethics of argumentation. Jürgen Habermas, starting from normative or regulative speech acts and offers of speech acts in the everyday life-world, and from agreement oriented actions, seeks to ground a discursive ethics by means of formal-pragmatic investigations and a "logic of moral argumentation." Furthermore, as an ethics of accountability, it should provide a satisfactory answer to the question of justice and of "the good life" as institutionalized morality.[1] All these cognitivist ethics proceed tacitly from the assumption of the universal reign of reason. But also the non-cognitivist ethics, such as Max Scheler's and Nicolai Hartmann's intuitionist ethics of value, as well as the emotivist and decisionist ethics are mostly concerned only with the conventional comportment of an agent.

We expect an answer to very different questions from a non-metaphysical ethics. How does a person become just? How does a person become one who loves his fellow-man, how does a person become one moved by compassion? This ethics is not only concerned with the question of how the claims to validity of moral judgments can be tested for their possibilities of attaining truth—as is largely the case in contemporary ethics—nor only with the question of the "universalizing" of particular conceptions and of the application of the general to any given situation (the question of "concretization"). This has been traditionally the work of judgment; in Aristotle, it was a question of the feasibility of an action on the basis of a consideration in which a concrete situation is related to what the virtuous person takes to be the just and proper thing to do. In the following studies, we shall neither discuss the extent to which Aristotle's concretion contained the logical structure of an inference, nor shall we deal with the related problem that is also posed in the critique of Kantian ethical formalism as that of "reason putting law to the test" (the Kantian formalism of duty). We are rather concerned with the possibility of a transformation of ethical comportment on the basis of an experience that arises out of emotion and thus plays a role in the formation of virtues, without, however, excluding reason in doing so. We do not conceive *reason* in the Aristotelian fashion of *prohairesis,* nor in such a way that its *telos* is composed by those Aristotelian virtues that were ultimately oriented towards the polis, the perfect form of the *ergon anthropinon* being, for Aristotle, a life devoted to *sophia* as the godlike *noesis noeseos.*

What is peculiar to, or distinctive about, a nonmetaphysical ethics would lie above all in the liberation from Weberian purposive rationality without a return to Aristotelian teleology, a liberation directed towards a rationality which recognizes another role for emotionality in the formation of virtues. Thus, the phenomenological descriptions undertaken in this book want to show that "purposive rationality" cannot lead to the formation of virtues. The question presents itself whether any type of rationality at all could achieve this on its own. Speculative pure reason once laid claim to encompassing and elevating all types of rationality. But it was founded on the assumption of an identity of thought and Being, in which thinking—ultimately in the form of reason as system—claimed to be able to rule all reality and to penetrate it completely. This claim to an absolute power of reason and its concomitant will to subordinate to itself every last nook of reality failed as a philosophical position when the limits of such an all-encompassing rationality began coming to the fore ever more clearly. This failure led to the insight that there are, particularly in the domain of human existence, basic modes that do not reveal themselves to a reason that has elevated itself to absolute spirit. The insight into the limitation of reason and spirit could have guarded man from the dangerous urge to a progressive rationalization of his life-world. But this did not happen because of the still predominant blind insistence on the convictions of the all-encompassing rule of purposive rationality. Still, in contemporary philosophy, the liberation from this and other traditional assumptions of metaphysics has opened up the possibility of posing new questions and of seeing traditional contents differently in a changed situation.

But can we today simply return to virtues? Plato taught that this was possible through knowledge. Aristotle stated that to knowledge must be added practice. Is it possible for us today to acquire this knowledge and develop our character in accordance with it? It is not, and for two reasons. First, because in antiquity and presumably in all our previous periods, the relationships that men bore their fellow-men were not governed by indifference to the extent they are today as a result of "scientification," technicalization, and the emergence of a "mass society." The person today who wants to show ethics the way to the regaining of virtues, must above all point to a phenomenon that is suitable for breaking through this indifference in a radical way. In no way should it be some far-fetched construction; it should rather spring from a state of affairs that belongs to our Being. To our Being belongs above all that we are mortal.

These essays will show how the individual can be transformed in the experience of mortality in such a way that the *measure for the capacity of com-passion* is disclosed as an existential possibility. As a force that has become operative, this measure—and this is our thesis—could develop his *ethos* in the virtues of sympathy, acknowledgment, and neighborly love to such an extent that he could participate sympathetically in the fate of others.

Let it be mentioned explicitly at this point that we are not concerned, in what follows, with presenting the history and the problems of theories of compassion; nor do we propose to analyze the different structure of meaning on the part of the phenomenon of sympathy as contrasted with the phenomena of justice, love, and neighborly love. Our question is directed towards the *genesis* of virtues in our life-world. Here, particularly in the first of the following phenomenological descriptions, the central problem is how the disclosure of the capacity for com-passion as a healing force could provide a measure.

For us, the capacity for com-passion belongs to the integral moments within the existential constitution of being-there, which, understood phenomenologically, is the phenomenon that reveals itself of its own accord, even if it is often hidden. Thus, the possibility of the capacity for com-passion appertains to each person and distinguishes the human being as a human being in this unfeeling universe. This is not belied by the fact that it is mostly not revealed in individual and social life. Because it belongs to the determination of man's Being, phenomenological philosophy has the task of revealing it as well as of describing the path of transformation on which it is disclosed and where it becomes operative. This is not equivalent to a teleological presentation of the realization of a potentiality.

How can the capacity for com-passion and its efficacy as an ethical force be characterized in greater detail in advance? Already we have to pay attention to the fact that the capacity for com-passion, as a phenomenon belonging to the Being of man, signifies an ability to share the suffering of others. It must not be equated with having compassion merely in the sense of changing mental states that can be described by psychology.[2]

If, however, the capacity for com-passion belongs to the constitution of Being of our existence and is precisely *not* operative for the most part in our daily life of indifference, the question arises as to how it can be revealed. It could take place on a path of transformation on which the person following it becomes aware of the limitation and transience of human Being in an attuned and intuitively rational way. This experience, which goes beyond the mode of Being of our everyday attunement, that is, indifference, makes it possible for the capacity for com-passion to be revealed and to become operative as a healing force, though not in a speculative and metaphysical way as in Schopenhauer's attempt to ground the principle of life in universal suffering.

For the one who passes through the path of transformation, the disclosure of the mode of Being of the capacity

for com-passion happens *at one* with the experience of the
other as *other,* more precisely as the other of *myself,* that is
to say: as the person whose Being constitutes a value in itself and who is given over to the same finitude as I am. For
as long as the force of the capacity for com-passion remains
operative in being-there, a person dwells in this transformed relation to the other and to all others, or to a communal group. He has shared, and shares, inasfar as it is
possible for him as a singular existence, in the weal and woe
and the pain of others. This phenomenologically verifiable
circumstance allows us to designate that operative healing
force terminologically as the "capacity for compassion."

This sharing in the fate of others in the light of the now
operative force of the capacity for com-passion can be further developed until it reaches the point where it is consolidated in forms that are given a priori as forms of
interhuman relations and which have traditionally been
defined as *virtues,* for example, acknowledgment, compassion, and neighborly love. Only the force of the capacity for
com-passion that has become operative enables these virtues to attain an intensity that distinguishes them essentially from all their configurations in the "mode of Being of
indifference."

III

The phenomenological descriptions of an ethics can
best be evaluated as such by presenting two examples. Admittedly, these can only prepare the exposition of a nonmetaphysical ethics concerning one's fellow-man and of a
social ethics. As the first example of a description of *ethos,*
we take a possibility of human comportment that allows
man to experience one side of his Being, the one that is
comprised by his *mortality.* We should like to show how an
attunement, namely, that of "horror," [*Entsetzen*] can bring
him before the fact of his mortality. Horror, and the fright
accompanying it, can dis-place him from all his habits and
set opinions, and can set him off on a path on which any

indifference is dissolved and destroyed. The guide on this path is not rationality but an ever-increasing emotion accompanied by a pre-predicative "understanding" that does not proceed by discursive inference though it still belongs to reason. The dissolution of indifference on this path is such that one learns to experience one's fellow-man, out of the capacity for com-passion, not merely as another one present to hand but as the "neighbor." This is the theme of the first of the following studies.

Not only our mortality, however, but also our *sociality* belongs to the configurations that make up the Being of man. The second study shows how also here—particularly today in the face of the possibility of total extinction—the attunement of horror can not only overcome indifference, as well as how other emotions can show the way to a "commitment" to the community, to an appropriation of social virtue whose source is likewise the capacity for com-passion. To be sure, in a state based on law and freedom our rationality must also be a determining factor.

The three subsequent investigations deal with our *life-world*. This is so permeated by scientific and technical "idealizations" that the real relations men bear to it can only be experienced in a concealed form. One does usually not perceive the "richness" which lies in the fact that man is able to exist in many different life-worlds "simultaneously" and "in succession," nor does one notice how the ethical, as capacity for com-passion, "colors" the various life-worlds. Both phenomena, the fact that we do not live in "one" world but in a plurality of worlds, and the power of the ethical were not hitherto the thematic object of the more recent discussions of the life-world.

CHAPTER 2

Ethos and Mortality

Perhaps the most important task facing those who are engaged in philosophical thought today is to search for an ethics that can provide a measure for responsible action to even those people who either can no longer find such a measure in the teachings of their religions, or who are no longer convinced by the metaphysical foundations of ethics. Unlike those who still dwell in the grace of faith and for whom the divine commandments also are still decisive as the contents of an ethics metaphysically conceived, all the people for whom these possibilities are closed off just live from day-to-day without orientation. Many people attempt desperately to find out if certain experiences are not possible which would afford a measure for responsible action without presupposing faith and metaphysics. We must emphasize that the search for "another" ethics is not motivated here by a position against the Judeo-Christian tradition, nor by an atheistic stance. On the contrary, nothing would be more desirable than a reassertion of the Judeo-Christian ethic in the face of the worldwide decay of many standards and the threats posed by technology and nuclear war.

Yet is it not our duty nevertheless to face up to the fact that precisely these developments have made the fundamental assumptions of metaphysics questionable and have shut off the dimension of the sacred in which alone a relation to a divine being can exist for faith? In the face of this distress, however, the question poses itself whether it is not possible and timely to seek the foundations of an ethics, foundations that rest on the possibility of transformations of our *ethos* by experiences of a sort which we can undergo in our own being and which lead to a measure for responsible action without presupposing either faith or metaphysics. This measure would have the same content as the metaphysically conceived ethics, so that a nonmetaphysical ethics could also be significant for those who believe. Only the configurations of the old *virtues* afford a motive for fending off the dangers threatening us and all subsequent generations, which many are calling into view in an incisive and convincing way today. These problems not only pertain to an ethics of neighborliness but to a social ethics as well, for both belong together.

I

Is there a possibility of a transformation of ethical comportment without the believing relationship to divine measures and without metaphysics? Does such a possibility exist in an experience which can lead to the revealing of a measure? If philosophy inquires without metaphysical presuppositions after the possibility of such an experience, should it not at first consider whether an entirely different essence of measure is at stake here than the one conceived by metaphysics?

We shall assume, in anticipation, that one of the essential features of a measure thought nonmetaphysically, as is the case for a metaphysically conceived measure, is the fact that it is binding on the grounds of "absolute certainty." Is there anything "absolutely certain" at all for the one who does not believe and who is no longer metaphysically oriented? The answer is an emphatic "yes." It is certain for that person, or at least it should be, that he is born as a *mortal*. Yet the fact of our own mortality possesses a curious "certainty" for us, for we refuse to believe it. It is not a question of death as the end of our life or as the decaying of our body. We can "experience" neither of these during our life. Nor is it a matter of death as the opposite of life, as a condition which the non-believer takes to be one of nothingness. It is rather death in the sense that we can experience it. Anyone can become aware of the fact that he is a mortal in the sense that from the moment of his birth and in every hour of his life he is "delivered over to death," and that it is also this which constitutes his *Being:* living, always already passing away in being-there, and in this sense to be "dying." But then the verb "to die", like the substantive "mortal," designates not only the event at the end of life, its last hour before passing over into death, but also the fact that in us, in our being-there, death is constantly, indeed hourly, at work. We can experience this continual passing away that is always already occurring. We can and should experience that precisely this, our mortality, is a constituent in the truth of our Being.

Yet how can it be thought that an experience of our own mortality could lead to the revealing of the measure for responsible action?

When we ask in this way we enter into the domain of possibilities of experience that have not been envisioned by the traditional methods of philosophical reason in its direction towards ultimate foundation—those of deducing, of dialectical presentation, or syllogistic proving in foundational relations. Although the so-called other thinking of contemporary philosophy also proceeds rationally in its own way and gives great importance to the rational character of judgment, critical questioning, and the critically investigation of what lies behind appearances, in the path of experience that is to be described in what follows, and which admittedly pertains to only *one* layer of human Being, emotionality or affectivity plays a significant role. With very few exceptions—Spinoza and Hume, for example—the philosophers of the tradition have conceived the affective life as irrational and destructive, and even today it remains largely neglected in the contemporary projects of ethics. In contrast to this, we want to pay attention to the possibility of experience that lies in the domain of the emotional: in our attunement [*Gestimmtheit*] and our disposition [*Befindlichkeit*]. Additionally, this may contribute to the important question for contemporary philosophy about the relation between the leading conception of rationality (namely the rationality of means and ends) and emotionality.

What do attunement or disposition mean? Edmund Husserl has shown that there is an original dimension of pre-reflexive, pre-predicative understanding that precedes cognition. One of the merits of Heidegger's *Being and Time* is that he was able to reveal that there is pre-predicative understanding only in conjunction with the "mood in which one finds oneself." This original understanding is accompanied by a disposition or an attunement, which is an originary disclosing—but also a closing off—that precedes all predicative understanding and volition and that opens up or disguises man's own Being. Furthermore, because being-in-the-world is an equally original part of the determination of man's Being, his disposition or his attunement simultaneously reveal his world to him as a whole with each and every thing within it.

If, for example, I step out of the house on a spring morning, my joyous attunement discloses my own being as well as the whole of my world to me as joyous, in such a way namely that within this world the things and my fellow-men strike me as full of joy. They do not reveal themselves to me in this way because I have a representation of them or because of a logical inference, but because of the disclosing character of my attunement, of my joyful Being and being-in-the-world that is attuned in such a manner. A sudden change of attunement can also transform ourselves and everything about us as if at a stroke. Attunement or disposition is indeed a transforming force. It is this transforming force—and in this respect we go beyond Heidegger—that can set us off on the path of further attunements, which transform themselves of their own accord.

As is well known, Heidegger attempted to show in *Being and Time* that anxiety is the basic attunement of Dasein. When one is prepared for the experience of anxiety—anxiety about oneself, which is at the same time an anxiety about one's being-in-the-world—then one can become "authentic." Heidegger, however, did not see that within the element of attunement or of disposition—and thus of the emotional—a transformation is possible in a completely different direction: not towards an authenticity that shuts itself off from other people but towards the old virtues of love, com-passion, and justice.

With regard to the essence of such a transformation it must be taken into account that we always already live in a communal world in which we are together on the basis of actions and interactions, habitualities and communication of manifold kinds that fold into each other and complement each other, and that come into play in the pre-existent domain of language and culture, and of the connection to things and to nature. The structures of this community are as such invariant. They remain constant regardless of any transformation according to attunement. In contrast to this, the changing attunement, which is changing, affects the entire "content" of the relations within which the one who changes moves.

Our thesis is this: within the domain of our attunement, our disposition, our emotional life, there is the possibility of a *Path* that can lead us from the experience of our own mortality to those matters that constitute the basis for the old virtues. For attunement is not, as Heidegger saw, only disclosing and concealing; the attunement that issued from the experience of our own mortality has the power to start us off on a path that leads to these virtues. How can the possibility of this path be shown?

II

Instead of proving by inference, the nonmetaphysical method of a phenomenological-hermeneutical description can reveal how the experience of one's own mortality can dispatch one on a path in the course of which a certain "healing" force—the capacity for com-passion—becomes more and more operative. This could be the basis for the development of a nonmetaphysical ethics of neighborliness, which can exist beside the Judeo-Christian metaphysical ethics concerning one's fellow-man.

As already emphasized at the beginning of our first observations, the following description should by no means be misunderstood as a depiction of a factual occurrence. First, the issue will be to interpret the phenomenon of the experience of mortality itself. Then, for the further description, the question already formulated above will be our guide: What does the path look like on which man, after having experienced his own mortality, can finally achieve the greatest possible assuming of responsibility and the development of the virtues of sympathy, acknowledgment, and neighborly love? Thus, we do not claim that the experience of one's own mortality leads "automatically" to the path described in what follows. Completely different paths, which lead one away from that initial experience, are also possible, but they do not constitute our theme and would have to receive a separate phenomenological description in their own right. In answering our question concerning the path on which man can assume the virtues for himself, transformatively, we must strive not to posit the stations on this path arbitrarily but rather allow them to reveal themselves solely from man's Being.

Such a description is meaningful and effective only when that which we make visible phenomenologically is also seen by those who read the description, and precisely as that which reveals itself as a "phenomenon in its evidence." What is seen may not, however, be forced aside by received concepts or comparative representations.

Perhaps precipitated by some kind of experience, but also wholly unexpectedly, the meaningful content can come forth and reveal itself to me, horrifyingly, which can be expressed in the sentence: I am continually passing away, or: I am continually dying. It is this matter which, when it overcomes me, can force me toward an intuition of death as the force which allows my Being to pass away constantly, hourly. It is this matter which sets me beside myself with horror which dis-places me, in the true sense of this word, from all the familiar relations and habits pertaining to myself, to the things in my environment, and which above all ex-pels me from the everyday modes of

being-with my fellow-men. The occurrence of such expul-
sion or dis-placement is accompanied by a corresponding
attunement which we know as the feeling of being beside
ourselves with horror, not of [*Entsetzen*], the anxiety that
for Heidegger constitutes the basic disposition of Dasein. It
is this dis-placement which brings everything that is fixed,
all unshakeable opinions and ideas, into flux and which,
above all, brings about the disintegration of that feature
by which modern philosophy characterizes the subjectivity of the subject: the volitional planning capacity for self-
determination.

Let us bring this into view more precisely. Hitherto I
was conscious of myself, even if only vaguely, as a being
who, despite the mortality lying in my Being, lived in the
curious security of being of a nearly "eternal kind of being."
My fellow-men, the Others of whom I was aware through
manifold interactions and communications in the common
life-world, in my view, possessed the mode of Being of what
is also "present to hand," which differs only very little from
that mode of Being which things had for me. The disposition that determined the relation I had hitherto maintained towards the Being of my fellow-men—and it is of
great importance that precisely this be seen—was one of
an *indifference* very impoverished of feeling.

Is it not primarily the indifference destitute of feeling,
the emotional situation of our relations to our fellow-men,
which hinders and blocks off all possibilities of friendly
comportment? An emotion, an affect that would strike one
radically in one's innermost Being, could be the beginning
of a path that breaks through this indifference and leads to
a transformation of the relations to one's fellow-men. Because of this, we concentrate on a path that begins with
this radical affect, horror, knowing full well that there are
other paths. What happens when my attunement of indifference is transformed into that of horror, and how does my
mortality then come forth, through further emotions as a
"truth of my being"?

It was not through a volitional and rational reflection
that I suddenly became aware that and how death, which is

constantly and hourly jutting into my Being, is at work and is allowing me to pass away. All of a sudden, through a change in my attunement, I experienced myself as being underway on a calamitous path. Here it is necessary to see clearly and to follow the experience. I, the one who has encountered the fact of his mortality ineluctably, experience further, with persistent fright and horror that I am indeed totally alone on this path, and that I must pursue it all by myself. For the particularity of the disposition of horror lies in the fact that this horror has radically thrown me back upon myself so that I feel totally forlorn, and experience that I must take my continual passing away upon myself without any help. I have no control over this fright that progressively thrills through me, and over the horror it caused, which is in sharp contrast to my rational reflections, which I can assume or reject of my own volition. As a new attunement, it is the fright that sets me beside myself with horror which is able to supersede the attunement of indifference completely, and which leads to that of utter loneliness and helplessness. Horror, forlornness, and helplessness are the attunements that have now replaced indifference and that unmask my naive security as mere illusion, as only a veneer.

We now see more clearly. It is not only the condition of the radical disintegration of all my fixed attitudes but also the emotions of forlornness and helplessness that were called forth by the horror filled with fright; it is this whole disposition, this emotional element, within which further transformations can take place. Through this the mode of Being of my fellow-men is changed increasingly for me, and my relation to them can be transformed into a one in which they actually become *others* for the first time, that is—in the true sense of this word—others in, and on the basis of, the relation to me as the "One". Thus they become "others of myself," as Hegel calls this relation in the *Phenomenology of the Spirit*.

A new stretch of the path of experience begins with that attunement of forlornness and of helplessness. In order to see this, we must call to mind that each of us, whether or not we are in the attunement of indifference, lives in a social life-world in which precisely as social beings we all speak to each other and listen to each other. Sociality belongs to our essence just as mortality does. Thus, the yearning for community can awaken precisely when the horror felt at constant dying drives a person into the mood of forlornness and of isolation. There can be a point at which he can no longer bear the attunements of forlornness and helplessness, precisely because he is a social, that is to say, a speaking and listening being. Although they are capable of driving him into total resignation and despair, indeed even to suicide, the desire for community can still assert itself. Then the moment arrives in which—perhaps only in a silent way—he implores his fellow-men for help, begs for their attention, and hopes that the other will approach him as he approaches the other.

The mode of being which others have for me changes radically precisely through this. If they were previously experienced with indifference as being also "present to hand," how they have become those who could help me, become "helpers in time of need." This transformation has not taken place through the power of thought, nor through the work of the dialectical concept; it is rather a transformation within the domain of my affecticity, my emotional life, my attunement. It is this transformation that has brought me a new relation to my fellow-men.

But why do I hope at all that fellow-men could become "helpers in time of need" for me? Surely more than a changed emotional attitude, which could only be brought about by the power of attunements, is necessary for such a hope. Heidegger, as has been mentioned, shows that attunements are accompanied by a pre-predicative rationality. Aristotle, in the *Nicomathean Ethics,* comes to speak of a sort of rational perceiving that is intuitive and immediately knows what the right thing to do is in each case without having achieved this insight by means of rational argumentation. He calls this type of perception *"nous,"* (spirit) in contrast to sense perception. With this he wants to point to the fact that in the domain of ethical practice there is a "seeing" that illuminates and guides this practice rationally. Precisely this is the *insight* that accompanies all attunements. There is a non-sensuous perception in the form of a "seeing" that precedes all discursive consideration and each act of explicit judging. This seeing can be determined in traditional terminology as "reason which sees intuitively." It "sees" things and fellow-men differently in each different attunement. Thus, the emotional nearness to one's fellow-men as neighbors is matched by a certain way of seeing them in an intuitively rational manner.

The disintegration of set attitudes in myself and of any desire to assert myself in order to gain advantage over others, which issued from horror, as well as the condition of utter forlornness and helplessness, have freed me from the captivity of the limitations to which I was condemned by unfeeling indifference. Thus liberated, I "feel" not only closer to the other emotionally but I "see" him in a transformed way. Only when I have achieved a new sphere of freedom on that emotional path and have thereby opened myself up emotionally to an intuitively rational seeing, does my fellow-man actually reveal himself to my transformed attunement and my rational seeing as the "other of myself." All rational seeing, which perceives immediately, is accompanied by an equally immediate and rational "hearing." Because I have been transformed emotionally, I am not only able to *see* the other as my other in an intuitively rational manner but also to *hear* his *call* in an intuitively rational way just like the person who has actually been transformed into believing is capable of hearing God's call to him.

In which sense do we speak here of another's "call" to me? Let us recall once again: Every one is born as a speaking being and belongs to a world constituted by language. That is why I seek the other as a being capable, as I am, of speaking and also hearing, of "hearing" me and "listening" to me—not necessarily with the organ of hearing. If I am emotionally prepared, I hear and see the Other no longer in an indifferent attunement but in an attunement of extreme need. Thus, I hope to receive a "sympathetic" response from him. If I approach him emotionally, seeking this response, and in this attunement begin to see and hear in an intuitively rational way, then this is certainly not a quest for "communication," which only exists in the attunement of indifference, but an "appeal" to my fellow-men as the others of myself.

What do I hear and see in an intuitively rational way in this attunement of nearness? I see and hear that my fellow-man, although he is another person, is not a stranger. For I hear and see what I could never see and hear in the attunement of indifference, that he is given over to death from birth, just as I am, and has to pass away continually and hourly; that he is a "mortal" just as I am, that he, who became a helper in my need in my attunement of forlornness, just by his mere existence, equally needs my help and my approaching him in his distress; he is my neighbor as one who shares my fate; a neighbor who has just as much a claim to my help as I have to his. However, does he permanently become a "neighbor" in this sense merely through the fact that I have experienced him thus as one who shares my fate? This he can only become if my seeing and hearing have liberated themselves increasingly from the captivity of indifference and when a perhaps silent discourse has begun with him as the other of myself, and if I have thus learnt to experience him increasingly as my "relative" despite all the differences he embodies as a person.

Because my intuitively rational insight and my intuitively rational hearing of the call the other addresses to me are prepared by emotional attunement and remain accompanied by it, no further factor needs to be introduced in order to explain how my insight and my hearing of the calls of others are turned into actions. While ethical theories, which take maxims, imperatives, and rules as their starting point, have to explain elaborately how an individual comes to acknowledge these rules—which possibly contradict a person's own inclinations—the one who, having been transformed emotionally, has seen the Other through rational seeing and hearing as the "Other of himself" and has apprehended his call, readily acts according to this insight and to this call, that is to say, he assumes the responsibility connected with this.

As I have now experienced for the first time the other in the Being that determines him as Other, a breach is made in my indifferent attunement. That this was at all possible, that I am at all able to encounter the other in this wholly transformed manner, cannot for its part be explained by the mere fact that it has taken place. It is founded as a possibility to be seized in the constitution of Being of Dasein being-there itself. Thus, the experience of the other as the other of myself, which motivates my turning towards him with sympathy, points to a structure of Being on the part of Dasein being-there that is revealed *at one* with that experience and which becomes operative in my facing the other. I call this possibility, grounded in being-there, or comporting oneself in an attuned and intuitively understanding manner towards the other and others, of partaking in their fate, the capacity for com-passion. It is the capacity given to man of being able to share the suffering of life as such, and thus of that, which I have in common with the other and all others: the transience that is part of life. For—and one should make this clear to oneself again and again—on this one planet in a universe devoid of feeling, there is a being that carries within it this possibility of feeling com-passion.

Not too long ago, Nietzsche indicted the feeling of compassion as a prejudice deriving from Christian morality. Schopenhauer was moved profoundly by the possibility of being compassionate; in his view, however, this found its adequate expression only in the basic attitude which, seeing through the *principium individuationis*, gives up the will to live altogether.

In contrast to this, on the basis of the analysis we have carried out, we see that the capacity for com-passion, revealed in Dasein being-there, expresses itself as a specific *force* that is at work in the concrete relations of sympathy. The comportment in sympathy, which is imbued with this force, can develop itself further to the point at which it consolidates itself in attitudes of character. These are the forms which for their part are traced out a priori as possibilities for community with fellow-men, which being-there Dasein in the mode of Being of indifference, however, does mostly not seize. They are the forms in which I remain related to the others in an attuned and intuitively rational way, as is the case above all with acknowledgment, compassion, and neighborly love. These forms, which the philosophical tradition from antiquity has sought to determine as virtues, are able to attain their full, consolidated development by the force of the capacity for com-passion that has become operative and is imbuing them. Here, this force means more for them than a mere awakening and enlivening. In radiating through them, it gives them intensity and the dimension in which they, for their part, determine the life of a person as one who acts in a responsible way. In a word, the operative force of the capacity for com-passion is the *measure* that determines the individual forms of acknowledgment, sympathy, and neighborly love through and through.

Turning with sympathy to a fellow-man as the "other of myself" proceeds through many degrees. The first one is that I *acknowledge* him as "my equal." Actual acknowledgment based on personal justice only exists when I myself am pervaded totally in my whole Being by the feeling that my fellow-man is in his essence ultimately like me. The difference between my person and the other becomes less significant for me as the attunement grows stronger in me, which can already be experienced in this first form of taking a sympathetic interest.

It is not through the development of the "concept of acknowledgment" as in Hegel's *Phenomenology of the Spirit,* nor through a generosity of tolerance instilled in me by reflection—which is always also determined by a feeling of superiority—that I become one who acknowledges the other in a really just way, but only on a path of emotion that starts with the attunement of horror at my own mortality and leads to an actual transformation of my Being in the element of attunement accompanied by insight, and intuitively rational seeing and hearing, a transformation that is also an unfolding of what characterizes man as a human being above all.

Admittedly, the transformation into a just person, who acknowledges the other permanently on the basis of justice, does not take place in a single blow. What was experienced in the immediately rational seeing and hearing, and, at first, in the horrifying encounter with one's own mortality, must be developed into a perduring character. This stabilization is possible precisely because, as we have seen, the emotional transformation, which is permeated with the force of the capacity for com-passion, calls forth, and thus also includes, rational seeing and hearing of the other. What would otherwise be a fleeting mood can be developed into certain attitudes towards others. There is a path of education in the human domain of freedom, which is disclosed emotionally. But in order to keep this open and to consolidate it in terms of character, other powers are needed, in particular those which traditional ethics has determined as judgment and as the critical faculty and which contemporary theories of action designate with different names. These powers are of course needed in responsible relations to our fellow-men, in our relation to our communities, as fellow-citizens of a society and a state, as well as in our relation to the environment. Still, with regard to all human powers based on rationality, the experience of one's own mortality which enabled the other to become "my other," the sharer of my fate, remains at work in the background.

Likewise, the only one who feels genuine *compassion* is the one who, through the dissolution of all presuppositions, has come to see and to hear, in such a way that he apprehends the claim of the other that calls him to assume his responsibility so as to suffer with all others even if he does not know them personally. Love, in the determinate sense of neighborly love, springs up in man according to our description of the path of experience when, having undergone the experience with his own mortality, he pursues the transformative path all the way—an experience that made possible the seeing and hearing of the other as fellow-man.

We can speak of a character-forming path that passes through stages, because sympathetic justice, sympathy, and neighborly love are borne by the same attunement in increasing degrees of power, and permeated by the same force of the capacity for com-passion.

III

But what about the other himself? Let us call him *B* as distinct from *A* of whom we have spoken hitherto. How can *A* assume that *B* will also not remain indifferent and will no longer merely regard *A* as present-to-hand, as if he were a thing?

But is it really the case that the fellow-man, *B*, to whom *A* actually turned, whom he acknowledges through the force of the capacity for com-passion, and for whom he feels sympathy or whom he loves as a neighbor, remains untouched by this attention? A phenomenological description cannot prove with the necessity of the concept, it cannot show, as Hegel could with the "concept of acknowledgment," that the relation of master and slave must come forth in the element of consciousness as if of its own accord to "unity in its doubling," and that, already on the first stage of this path, the slave must become the master of the master. However, a phenomenological description is possible of this fact that, for example, the hitherto unacknowledged *B* is already transformed merely through the fact that a fellow-man, *A*, now acknowledges him, without requiring of *B* himself any contribution to this. As an acknowledged person, he no longer experiences himself as an indifferent object of the person acknowledging him or even as an unfree person subordinate to him but rather, in the freedom that belongs to him essentially by simply being human—which means that *B* experiences himself as being equal in essence with *A*, who freely acknowledges him. And is not the same true of compassion and love? Do not *A*'s compassion and love touch *B* without direct influence? *B*, who is empathized within *A*'s compassion, who is loved in *A*'s neighborly love, experiences himself, surely, as being worthy of compassion and love and merely through this the willingness and desire could unfold in him to correspond to this never before experienced dignity. At any rate, *A*'s compassion and love lead him to a self-respect that could not only free him from the attunement of indifference towards himself but also could transform him into a disposition that could be developed further.

B, who is empathized with, has, as can be seen, already experienced the disintegration of fixity, of all presuppositions, through the suffering which called forth *A*'s compassion. That is to say: that capacity for transformation is already within him that in *A* did not come alive until he experienced horror at his own mortality. Still, which direction, more precisely, should *B*'s transformation take, so that he too could become a compassionate person and not only towards the one *A?* In *A*, the transformation went in a direction that brought him to an awareness of the truth of his Being, of his mortality, and then led him to the insight that all others are given over to death, that they are mortals, and thus share the same fate. The fact, however, belongs equally to the truth of human Being that everyone is given over to the possibility of being or becoming suffering. No one is impervious to the fate, that he might be dispatched into suffering sooner or later. Indeed, *B*'s readiness to share suffering not only with an *A* but with every other one is equally anchored in the Being of man as the fact that he must die. The explicit development of com-passion on the part of *B* could be "sparked" by *A*'s attention.

Precisely in this phenomenon it can be shown that and how there is always already an "attuned commonality," an "attuned intersubjectivity," which allows for an even more fundamental explanation of the question why *B*, touched by *A*'s compassion, can in turn become a compassionate person for all others. The ontological determination of "being-with" does not capture this issue if being-with is thought without that disposition which inspires and enlivens it, and which we have called "sympathizing with" [*Anteilnahme*]. Only sympathizing being-with grounds true intersubjectivity, which is also not articulated, for example, in an "under-standing" relation but rather in an always differently attuned "encounter"—in particular the encounter out of compassion, a sympathizing involvement that goes so far as to "share" the suffering that does or can afflict us all. The fact that this sympathizing involvement can in turn transform B into a compassionate person without further ado, makes it clear that and how attuned commonality belongs to the essential constitution of human Being. That this attuned community exists, that participation in it can bring the essence of man to fulfillment or completion, is shown even more clearly in the phenomenon of neighborly love. Before we investigate this, we must bring up a reservation that could already arise at this point become more pressing in the subsequent expositions. If B in turn has become a compassionate person through A's compassion, if the attuned community of participation in which B already finds himself actually only needs to be brought to a further realization, then does this not mean that the path of experience presented above, which began in A with the experience of his own mortality, is not at all necessary for B in his transformation into a compassionate person? We will attempt an encounter with this important reservation below.

Does the love A bestowed upon B as his "neighbor" spark in B a readiness for neighborly love? Here as well the precondition is that a liberation of B from the indifference that has ruled him up to now must first of all be achieved. The awareness that it is he who was chosen by A's neighborly love may indeed suffice to tear B out of his indifference. In addition, the fact that he has become the other of A and A's striving to evoke a response in him may have already effected in him the experience that he always already lives in a world he shares with everyone because he is a being who can give a response, a speaking being who belongs to a world constituted by language. And it is above all this attuned community in which he—as a speaking being—is always already involved, like out of which he could answer in "corresponding" attunement, just like a "helper in time of need" responds.

Furthermore, is it not the case that *B*, precisely because he belongs to an attuned community of speakers and listeners from the outset, is never merely "dumb?" Does he not constantly "speak" to every other, though in a soundless way? Does he not constantly address a call to each and every one, though tonelessly, a call that says: notice me, acknowledge me, relieve me from my loneliness, have compassion for me, love me? *B*, speaking soundlessly in this manner, waits for this call to be heard. He waits for neighborly love, he expects compassion. If these are bestowed upon him, something completely new occurs in the element of his disposition.

The fulfillment of the call of the person waiting for neighborly love releases joy in him, joy at having been heard, at having been listened to. He is suddenly in an "elevated mood." Joy, like anxiety, is universal. Whoever is in a joyous mood, is happy about everything, about the fact that he is there at all, that he exists and that the other exists as well, where this "that . . . exists" encompasses the Being of the world, the totality of of beings and every that is. The fact that joy is universal means something further. Joy "is infectious." Joy—as the poet says and as the song sings—is the "beauteous divine spark"; it is joy which, as the "daughter from Elysium," makes "brothers" of all men wherever it dwells. It has the effect that attuned community comes forth and can be experienced as the element in which each person is the other's fellow-man. Joy, which seeks to hold a "joyous conversation" with all Others, would that not be neighborly love of one's fellow-man, the highest transformation of which man is capable?

However, can this joy that *B* feels as the result of the fulfillment of his appeal, and even that joy which is only released by "infection," bring about an attitude in relation to all others, that forms an enduring basis for character and which alone may actually be called "neighborly love?" For does that joy not pass quickly, particularly in the joyless and cumbersome ways of our living together in which each of us must play his everyday role? Is not a more thorough-

going experience required in order to lead to character-
forming attitude of neighborly love? In an onto-theological
manner, metaphysical ethics could take the highest being—God—and His love as the guiding measure for a continual renewal of human neighborly love. [This path is
closed off for a non-metaphysical ethics.

   Our question at this juncture is how then a love for
one's fellow-man, which issues merely from the joy at an
appeal that has been listened to, can be consolidated.] Is
there a way from that harmonious mood of agreement to
the attunement that gains a steadiness, capable of building
character, from the experience of one's own mortality? This
path would doubtlessly only exist if the joyful person experienced a lack, as it were, in his own skin. The possibility of
such an experience exists. We see it in the fact that all joy
still has the tendency to change, to turn around suddenly
into a mood that begins to undermine the joy. Is it not the
case that precisely when the joyous person yields emphatically and indiscriminately to his neighborly love in a single blow, the experience of the transience of such joy can
abruptly overcome him? Is it not the case that precisely out
of this attunement of joy the attunement of *melancholy* can
grip him, the melancholy that befalls the whole person and
makes him perceive the grief that lies over him and everything that is?

   It is easy to see how this attunement of melancholy becomes one that rules *B,* disposition similar to the one we
described as coming over *A* with horror and engendering in
him the experience that he is dying continually, hourly,
delivered up to death as a "mortal." If this befalls *B* in a
similar way in the attunement of melancholy, then his
transformation to neighborly love could result from such
an experience on a path resembling the one *A* passed
through—that is to say, on a path on which the other could
be experienced as the other of himself and on which, at one
with this, the force of the capacity for com-passion could be
disclosed revealed. Neighborly love, which led to a radical
transformation of *B* on the basis of this experience, would

become a *hexis* and would possess a character-forming quality because it would now have a foundation in the truth of his Being.

Thus also, for the person who is addressed by compassion and in turn becomes compassionate, his readiness for compassion is ultimately only strengthened by the fact that he learns to experience suffering on earth as a form of his having to die constantly. Only when the experience of suffering as a way of constant dying is present will he also accept and learn to share with others what can befall him or man as such in the form of suffering and will have become a compassionate person.

IV

The path on which the experience of death brings about a "dis-placement" can have the result that *A* as well as *B* feel themselves *healed* from the attunement of unfeeling indifference. The convalescent and the healthy only experience themselves as convalescent or healthy when they begin to feel better or no longer feel ill at all, when they actually sense the "healing force" within themselves. The healing force that we sense is indeed at work as an absolute, unaccountable force. Even conservative orthodox medicine acknowledges that there may be a healing power in the physical domain which cannot be explained further. We can likewise thus assume that there is a healing force at work in the productivity of the human soul, though it must not be interpreted in a teleological-metaphysical way. It is already at work in those who are on the path of transformation, accelerating it, but above all it continues to be effective in those who are healed. This healing force as the disclosed possibility of the capacity for com-passion works as a "giving," as what "gives" in what is given to us, as a "bestowing." It bestows healing in that it gives itself stability as a healing force, by making itself firm and giving itself form in precisely those configurations, or virtues of just acknowledgment, compassion, and neighborly love.

One can also think of this movement of healing as that of a *nearness* becoming ever more intimate, or nearing the other in such a manner. One can see that these configurations also include the actual relation to one's fellow-man: *A*'s nearing *B* and *B*'s nearing *A* and all other *B*s. The connection with the other grows with the increase of *nearness*. It is only through the development of a nearness experienced emotionally and of an ever ready seeing and a hearing of the other that the other becomes one who is near to me, one who is nearest, my fellow-man [*Nächster*]. That is the beginning of a life that can develop relationships with many others, with many fellow-men who are near. At one with this grows the regard in which an individual holds himself. Certainly, each and everyone lives in the "consciousness," in the experience of the meaning of his living being, and this in manifold respects: in the experience of being the center of all action, in that of the urgent task of having to protect one's own being and to maintain it at any cost. However, this meaningful context of his own being does not emerge clearly before him until he is mirrored, as it were, in the other. From the nearness of the other grows, for the first time, the true regard for oneself. Thus it can be said that the actual experience of the radical finitude of one's own Being, which is constantly passing away, in the attunement of sorrow at this loss, is needed in order to experience the joy of one's own being-there, indeed to be able to experience the "miracle" of one's own Being on the path through, and with, the existence of the other as one who is near.

Now what constitutes the essence of a measure that is to be thought nonmetaphysically? Is the healing force, this measure in the form of love, sympathy, and acknowledgment a maxim, an imperative, or a standard—as in Kant—that man encounters as a command and that going beyond man's own measures, has the mode of being of "transcendence?" This question must be answered in the negative. The person taking measures, who has transformed himself, *dwells* in his measure. It encompasses him and determines him through and through. Yet these traditional essential

characteristics also hold for the nonmetaphysical essence
of a measure. The healing force and its forms are absolute
and absolutely certain. For the loving one, the one who is
compassionate and just towards his fellow-man, the other
is unconditionally a loved one, one to whom compassion is
shown, and one who is justly acknowledged. This absoluteness and this certainty also ground the decisive essential
feature of the nonmetaphysical essence of measure: its
binding force which is valid for all cases. It shares these
three essential features—absoluteness, certainty, and
binding force—with the traditionally conceived essence.

The measure that has resulted from the path that led
the person from the attunement of his mortality to the experience of the efficacy of the healing force, being nonmetaphysical, is a measure of responsible action that can be
experienced here on earth, and, as such, does not have its
immediate source in the divine being. As such it is a measure with which man can at any time "take measures" with
which he will be able at any time to accept or reject as *good*
or *evil* what his responsible readiness encounters. What do
we then mean when we speak of "good" and "evil", how is
the one who takes measures responsibly related to the
measure on the level of measuring, and what does "measuring" mean if man already "dwells" in the measure? For
the one whose whole Being, for example, is determined
by compassion arising out of the measure of the capacity
for com-passion, it immediately emerges as if of its own
accord obvious, without any special taking of measures,
how and with whom he will feel compassion. He knows immediately who and what accord with his compassion in
each case; he knows what is good in this sense of accordance and what is, contradicting the measure that dwells
within him, evil. As the poet says, "The good man in his
dark desire knows the right path full well." That, and how,
then, when applying these measures in a certain situation,
discursive and argumentative reason as judgment and as
our critical faculty play a role cannot, however, be eluci-
dated by us here. Only this much: it is reason borne by

emotion and by intuitively rational seeing and listening to the other and not a cold, calculating, and planning reason.

The phenomenological description of individual steps of the path on which an individual has transformed himself in his relation to another individual shows that this transformation *can* exist, though not that it *has to exist.* For the entire onto-theological tradition, God's love was the measure that must always be there. To be sure, man's constant passing away, which is founded in his Being as being mortal—is also "always" exists there, as long as he lives. But then again, the transformation of one's disposition into an attunement that ultimately carries the becoming operative of the healing force, as the measure determining him in the forms of love, sympathy, and acknowledgment *only* exists when he has actually experienced such a transformation within himself. The transformation can take place but he can then relapse into indifference; he can even oppose such a transformation from the outset consciously and with intent. The latter possibility presupposes, however, that the person understands himself as a "subject" in the modern conception, on whose will alone it depends that everything occurs according to his intentions. Has not precisely contemporary philosophy pointed to the reality of all that "happens to us" contrary to our projects? The insight on the part of philosophy and the social sciences into the "structure of occurrence" of our understanding and into the conditionality of our freedom has not been the only one to shake our self-understanding as an omnipotent subject. For, leaving this insight aside for the moment, do we not have to give heed to the actual events that "happen to us" and that everyone speaks about today? It has happened to us that our planet has shrunk; it has happened to us that all its inhabitants are exposed in common to the dangers of technology and of nuclear war. It is becoming increasingly evident that people are uniting in the West and in the East to struggle for the survival of humanity as a species and for the conservation of nature as their environment. Can we not see today that some groups in our pluralistic society, acting on insight into these dangers, have united into responsible communities? Has not that transformation of which we have spoken already taken place, underhandedly as it were?

And yet our description of the path of experience was intended to show precisely that the mere staring at death, regarded as the end of life, be it of the individual or of the species, does not bring about the actual transformation of man; only the experience the individual has with his own mortality, and which sets him off on the path at whose end his character changes and the virtues of acknowledgment of his fellow-man, compassion, and neighborly love have bodied forth in such a way that the other is really experienced as his "neighbor" can accomplish this. The mere closing ranks with people of the same political opinions is not, after everything we have said, sufficient for this. Nevertheless, today's tendencies and the readiness for solidarity and responsible action with respect to the great dangers facing humankind demands full attention on the part of the philosopher. The social and political problems connected with this, particularly in the current state of the world, would have to be investigated by the political sciences and, regarding their institutional order, by jurisprudence. A philosopher, however, must perhaps limit himself to pointing out emphatically that, in our largely secularized society, there is a need for orientation for responsible action, which has still not been discussed adequately. Furthermore, the philosopher can attempt to think another essence of measure and call people's attention to the possibility of disclosing such a measure, which can exist for the experience of a transformed person here on earth.

This was the aim of our observations. It was a question of revealing this possibility as such, and it cannot be emphasized enough that this is about an experience that does not have its foundation in something volitional, but rather in human Being itself, in mortality. From the Socratic question about the real world as opposed to the one of appearance, through Husserl's and Heidegger's view of the phenomenon to be disclosed, philosophical thought has al-

ways found the language and the concept for precisely that
which has the tendency to withdraw itself from "natural,"
everyday experience. The possibility of experience which
we have brought to light, in which the disclosure of the capacity for com-passion takes place and which withdraws
again and again, is that of the mortality that is always
one's own.

An "originary" experience is also the foundation for
Judeo-Christian ethics, an experience undergone only by
the few upon whom the divine grace of actual faith has been
bestowed; and yet this ethics has had, and continues to
have, a great influence also on those people who are not capable on their own of undergoing the original, truly transforming experience. Thus, the commandment of love indeed
lays claim to being universally observable and yet the
readiness and commitment of the individual in the inner
region of the heart, which issues from a transformation, is
actually still needed for its original realization. Such a
transformation, however, in contrast to the "commandments" that emerge from it, cannot be taught. Precisely in
this respect does it resemble the experience of mortality
and of the path proceeding from it that we have discussed.
One can always only point to this experience and to this
path anew. This is not contradicted by the fact that the
canon of commandments that issues from it, could be
teachable as a future concrete ethics; indeed it would have
to be taught in order to be able to assume an objective form.

At a time when the distress of a lack of orientation is
becoming ever greater through the increasing decline of
faith, while the readiness for responsible comportment on
the other hand seems to be growing, it should be significant
that, besides the Judeo-Christian ethics, virtues, whose
content certainly go back to it, like love, compassion, and
the acknowledgment of one's fellow-man, can be revealed by
a nonmetaphysical description of our *ethos* as forms of a
measure that exists *on earth*.

CHAPTER 3

Ethos and Sociality

I

The one who wishes to describe the human social *ethos* in a nonmetaphysical social ethics, must begin by screening off his view of himself as an individual in his relations with one particular or many other individuals. He does not ask how he, as an individual, could transform himself in his relationship to another individual in such a way that he would be able to experience the Other as his "fellow-man," this being the thematic object of the ethics concerned with one's fellow-man as one who is near. Proceeding from the fact that every person in her being is equiptimordially an individual *and* a member of a community, he will concentrate on describing his membership, his sociopolitical *ethos,* and will attempt to clarify what the sociality of man, of man *as a person,* consists of. The determination as "person" instead of "individual" designates her in her belonging to a community and a society. In doing so, he will pay attention to the particular features of the relation a person bears to her communities (for example to her family or to friends) as well as to determinate organizations, the state in particular. Above all he can discuss—and this is the theme of the following inquiry—whether, and how, a person can transform her indifferent everyday social way of life into one in which her sociality as such can be really achieved. The aim of our following observations lies in finding a measure for responsible social comportment that is able to determine one's life, fulfilling it wholly.

The method of this investigation is phenomenological in the sense discussed above. Thus, the following description does not claim to reproduce factual circumstances, but rather aims at the phenomenon of a possible path to an experience of sociality. In exploring this possibility, which is unfolded contra-factually here, we seek to give an answer to the question as to how man could come to experience social justice and social com-passion, as well as the question about the organization of a society in which these virtues could be realized. The manner in which both forms of the ethically relevant essence of man—to be an individual and a member of a collective, or a person—differ according to the particular cultural situation cannot be discussed within the limits of our inquiry. Still, the difference between the essential state of affairs of individual ethical comportment, and ethical comportment as a member of social group, will be significant for all that follows.

First, we shall attempt to determine the nature of the social relation, inquiring into the attunement that predominates in our everyday social life and into that which can tear us out of this vague everyday manner and awaken us to our true sociality.

Second, we shall investigate the aspect of the path leading to such a transformation that brings one to the virtue of social sympathy against the background of the capacity for com-passion that has become effective as a measure, and on which the individual would become fully conscious of his sociality. For the description of determinations of this path, we may glean a hint from traditional philosophical thought, in particular that of Hegel and Schelling.

In the last part of this inquiry, we shall redirect our gaze. If up to now we have investigated how a person can achieve the full appropriation of her social connection, we now ask about ideal organizational form of a state, in which the one who has developed the measure of the capacity for com-passion within himself, may live accordingly.

Even if nonmetaphysically conceived "essence of essence" differs in important basic characteristics from a traditionally conceived essence, the traditional distinction between the essential state of affairs of a formal and a material a priori may still provide a legitimate guideline for our analysis of the social relation—"a priori" understood here as what essentially "precedes."

One of these, the essential states of affairs constituting the *formal* a priori, consists of the fact that every person must necessarily and inescapably belong to a community and a society. We determine the structure of this essential state of affairs in greater detail as that of a formal *belonging* to a domain which, in its might, exceeds each individual person's possibilities of exerting an influence, and limits and determines these in many respects. Above all, it is inherent in this formal belonging that no one can lead the essence informing his membership, that is, his sociality, to his *telos,* or his goal, on the basis of his own resources. It holds for a non-theological, nonmetaphysical view of the state of affairs of this formal belonging that this not being able to realize oneself on one's own belongs to the essence of human sociality. It is already clear from this that there is no anticipatory, preemptive orientation towards a completely realizable fulfillment of sociality.

From a nonmetaphysical point of view, the social world in which each person lives as a member of a community or a society, is the *life-world* with its institutions. To this formal a priori belongs the essential moment aspect that the life-world is given in advance to whatever conduct within that world. Thus, there is much in the life-world that man finds as already there, which he needs, and whose availability, in anticipation, he relies on for self-preservation. The elementary provision of food and clothing would not be possible without a life-world in which this disposability has already taken place in advance. The child growing up in the life-world does not find it surprising that its elementary needs are always already satisfied from the outset. It is not very different in the case of the adult with respect to the conditions that are given in advance by custom and common practice as well as by law, culture, and all forms of state organization. He grasps them self-evidently as being given to him in advance, without taking their concrete content into account and moves within them solely because of their factuality. Above all, however, it is language into which each person must enter and in which he must grow up, whose meanings have accrued to him as if they were self-evident, and which guides him almost of its own accord not only in his interaction with others as individuals but also as a member of a political and social life-world.

A further aspect of the formal a priori, of belonging as the formal structure of membership, is the fact that it is always informed by an *attunement,* a particular way of being affected by a mood, in which every person "finds herself feeling" that he belongs to her community or society; this disposition in turn is accompanied by a particular sort of reason, an immediate, intuitively rational seeing and hearing. It is disposition and reason that characterize the "how" of a person's relation to her community or society, to her formal a priori.

In order to really discern this "how" of relating to a collective, we must also characterize the material a priori of a person's sociality as that which precedes concretely in terms of content. As we have stated, we proceed from the insight that our world has the character of a life-world. Concretely and in terms of content, a life-world for Husserl was the sphere "which presents itself to us on the basis of previous experience,"[1] the sphere which, in its historical character of having become what it is,"is always already there, without one doing anything, without turning one's view to seize upon it, without any awakening of our interest."[2]

It is the "world of experience,"[3] not only in the sense of an everyday *praxis* of life as "setting to work on something" but also precisely in its "spatio-temporal horizon,"[4] as the world of created cultural goods, works of art, and, the organization of the society organized as a state. Other configurations of social control such as the organized churches also belong to this, as do the individuals who bear this commonwealth.

Without having to commit ourselves to the constitutional problematic of Husserl's phenomenology, we consider it advisable to take our starting point in Husserl's determination of the life-world because we may thus avoid the conceptual distinction of a sphere of subjectivity from that of objectivity. The life-world relation to the world seen from a nonmetaphysical point of view is that of *dwelling* concretely in it. Dwelling in the life-world characterizes for us the material a priori of the "how" of sociality. Thus, we shall now also utilize the determination of *belonging* employed materially in the description of a person's social *ethos* in order to designate her social being in the collective of an institutionalized and organized society. Here the many modifications of this material belonging, according to the configurations of the particular institutions and organizations, would have to be unfolded. It is, however, not our task to follow these up individually. Our question is, rather, whether, and how, attunement and disposition, together with a rational immediate seeing and hearing, determine the material belonging as well.

In this connection, what do attunement or disposition together with a type of "understanding" mean as basic modes that contribute to bearing the belonging to a community or to a society? Proceeding from Heidegger's insights in *Being and Time,* we view attunement as the expression of "one's mood"; but, in contrast to Heidegger, we take "understanding" to be the carrying out of an intuitively realized seeing and a hearing.

We must now ask ourselves whether attunement and intuitively rational seeing and hearing are given to man as possibilities of awakening to the real Being of her membership and sociality? Are they aspects of the formation of her social character? One may assume everything appears to point to the fact that our belonging in the social world maintains itself in the attunement of a disinterested indifference, unless we stand in a pronounced disinclination to our community, have become alienated from it or, counterwise, unless we are decidedly committed to it. Furthermore, let us call to mind that within every life-world there is an order of Being which pertains to all relations— those of law, positively enforced regulations, morality, and religious dogmas—in short: the common culture and everything that is sedimented and that can always be revived anew by life-world comportment. How can our vague everyday disposition be characterized in greater detail with respect to this order? Psychoanalytic reflections have shown in their own way how egocentrically the individual lives within the order that preserve his existence. Often our attunement only respects order *nolens volens* because of its coercive character. Often, even, the indifference hides a striving to misuse the order, which is after all meant to serve the well-being of the entire society, for highly personal needs. As far as its fundamental attunement is concerned, this comportment often has the character of a pronounced enmity against society, which comes to the fore pronouncedly as such in times of social crisis. In cases like that, society is usually not the only enemy to be fought; rather, it becomes obvious that relations between individuals, are also marked by a latent readiness to engage in a *bellum omnium contra omnes*. In this relation between disposition and the order of the life-world it becomes clear that, in reality, belonging is usually not *oriented indifferently towards* commonality. Yet, it sociality is constituted both formally and materially in a belonging based on commonality, then the state of affairs we have described, which is often given de facto, has to be determined as a form of *privation* of fulfilled material belonging. In this privative form, the *societas*—on whose well-being the fate of the individual after all depends—and the claims it makes on the individual, as in the case of the demands by the state of its citizens, are "overlooked." One faces the interests of the community as such with indifference.

Thus, the question poses itself: as to how can this private form of belonging be superseded? How can the everyday indifference and self-interest in the social domain be overcome at all? It is not difficult to conceive that this is what happens in the case of catastrophes, war, or in a natural occurrence such as an earthquake. Then an individual is seized by moods that lift him from his asocial being and his insipid everyday attunement of indifference and self-

centeredness, suddenly bringing home to him his membership, his material belonging to a community such as the
family, friends, a people, and a society, or state. The mood
that lifts one out of oneself is accompanied by an intuitively
rational seeing and hearing, an intuitively rational insight
into say, the consequences of a situation of war or of a natural catastrophe. And it is accompanied by listening to the
claims that the community and society address to each person and which a person is able to apprehend. Thus, belonging and sociality come to the fore. A material commitment
to the collective with which every person is necessarily connected a priori can develop from this.

Admittedly, we have not yet achieved much with this
provisional result, for we are looking for a measure for responsible action, whose effectiveness is precisely not limited to extreme situations in social life, but which can
determine a life and completely pervade it.

Thus, we must ask: Which transformation would bring
about the complete emerging of the *common character*
based in fulfilled formal and material belonging from the
withdrawal that is so dominant today? We should like to direct ourselves at first to the metaphysical tradition. Did
metaphysical thought know of a similar problem? And how
did it conceive the actualization of the socially common?

II

It may perhaps be said that the greatest achievement
of metaphysics and of the Western mind in general lies in
the fact that it has struggled through to the insight that
freedom, properly understood, forms what is common to all
men and what must be brought to realization. It is the
sense of freedom whose concept was presented in world history by the French Revolution and then philosophically by
Kant and German Idealism. In this attempt at a synthesis
of the classical determinations of the *polis* with Stoic and
Judeo-Christian-Protestant thoughts, and with the Kantian and Fichtian moral philosophy, which he developed

further. Hegel determined freedom in the *Philosophy of Right* as what is common to all men, and conceived its highest form of realization as "absolute morality."

Excursus

In Hegel's early writings from the Frankfurt and Jena period up to his late works, a distinction can be made between how, on the one hand, he conceived the relation of one individual to another and, on the other hand, the relation of the one to his "we," his community and his society. This corresponds to our distinction between a description of *ethos* as the foundation of an ethics of neighborliness and of *ethos* as the foundation of a social ethics. Determinations that only pertain as such to the relation of one individual to another individual are found primarily in Hegel's later works, though they are usually presented in such a way that they at once pass over into a determination of the relation of the individual to the universal. Can be explained by the fact that Hegel, in taking over Aristotle's determination of *ethos,* which was based solely on the *polis,* was attempting to fundamentally overcome the Kantian view. For Kant, freedom was the transcendental determination of the individual consciousness. It is this alone that can become "free" in the "realm of ends," overcoming natural constraint. In contrast to this, for Hegel, freedom of the individual is precisely only possible through the fact that he overcomes his individuality and reaches freedom in the consciousness of his unity with the people, the class order, and with the institutions of the state. Freedom only exists for Hegel in its fulfillment in institutions of the spirit of the people. The elevation over the natural element in man, his desires and his drives, takes place in such a way that the freedom of the individual supercedes itself as a moment of the spirit of the people and of its "will." Put more precisely, the moral consciousness of the individual does not disappear but "supercedes and conserves itself" in a commonality that which, for Hegel, constitutes true or absolute morality. As moral substance, it lies in the mores, the religion, and all other institutions of a people in unity with an "educated self" which has come forth, through a history of education, out of the bondage to natural determinations and drives, in particular in drives in such a way that the individual has ultimately become an "educated self" or a "substantial self" that has relinquished all determinations of individuality.

In our own efforts to provide a description of a social *ethos* it is important that the above held for Hegel in all the stages of the development in which the individual will becomes the general will or a substantial subject, and that substance, for its part, emerged as a result of this out of this development as "self-like." For Hegel, clearly at any rate in the early works, this happened through a single principle: the "principle of acknowledgment," which is "itself the immanent structure of the principled."[5]

We cannot, nor do we need to, discuss in detail how this principle can be revealed in the *Phenomenology of Spirit*. It will have to suffice when we note that the movement of acknowledgment, as far as its structure is concerned, in losing oneself in the other, which Hegel also calls "being-outside-oneself," and in its negation of self-assertion or "being-for-itself" against the other, can always be shown to be a question of the coming forth of a common consciousness, of the coming forth of the "we" from the relation of one individual to another. In the presentation of the genesis of a "we," Hegel did not, as Sartre did, operate with a "triadic" concept but rather with a twofold concept.

What is common to all men, however, as is shown in the *Philosophy of Right* and in the *Phenomenology of Spirit,* is at first "withdrawn," to speak in our terminology, and is exposed to the danger of withdrawal again and again on the path to its realized form. Schelling had an even deeper insight into this condition when he wrote in the treatise on freedom: "The unruly force always lies at the base as if it could break through once again, and nowhere does it seem as if order and form were original forces, rather that something which was originally unruly has been brought to order."[6]

We have already noted for our part that behind the everyday, apparently completely disinterested indifference, there often lies a highly interested selfish emotion that is inimical to society and that would potentially be ready to engage in a *bellum omnium contra omnes,* that is, if the law and established moral norms did not prevent it. In this lies the *partial* withdrawal of our real Being. We have already described this possibility. And no reminder is needed today of Schelling's insight into a Being wholly threatened by chaos. We *know* that through a nuclear war a *total* withdrawal can come about of the socially common based on both formal and material belonging. This is not a fantastic construction; it has become an issue for phenomenological description today that we encounter, or rather should encounter, what threatens to befall us in the attunement of horror and in the intuitively rational seeing and hearing that accompanies it. Could this horror not grip the one who is still living in the traditional forms of order in such a way that the indifference and the selfishness with regard to all relations in society and the particular will that is hidden beneath this indifference and that is only directed towards one's own interest, can cancel themselves and thus lead to the path towards a fulfilled belonging on the basis of community? This means nothing less than that precisely today has become visible the possibility of taking the path from indifference to fulfilled sociality.

What course would this path run through? Would we not leave the domain of phenomenological description in attempting to describe it? This seems not to be the case if we direct our investigation to those states of affairs that can be revealed as possible in the Being of man on the individual stages of the transformatory path.

The attunement of an indifference governed by selfishness gives way at first to another attunement, namely fear of the insurgence of violence in the form of a nuclear war or a nuclear catastrophe. Particular interests would be pushed into the background with ever greater force by precisely this attunement. Through this, stages of emotions becoming ever more intense would disclose a domain that would be free of selfishness and indifference. In this, always on the basis of these emotions, the reason of a directly intuitive kind of "perceiving" insight remains at work. Here we have a seeing, and a hearing of the call of the community, which now awaken as care for the well-being of the community.

On this path that transforms man and his sociality, two things—to recall Hegel's *Phenomenology of Spirit*— would have to take place. The first is a *generalization* of all that which comportment in the life-world has sedimented in the form of norms of self-interest. Everything inherited, traditional, as well as every newly-acquired, antisocial attitude would have to be overcome both on an emotional and on an intuitive-rational level. Whatever determined a "false" consciousness directed towards self-interest through "overlooking" and "not listening to" the claims of the community would have to be transformed into an attitude that serves the collective and which is in this sense "generalizing." Hand in hand with this process of an increasing "becoming general" of the "I," the attuned intuitive-rational seeing of what community really is and the correlative hearing of its claims would have to be one of *interiorization*. On this path, hanging on to things that only serve particular interests would have to be overcome in favor of an interest in the general well-being so that the individual, after he has liberated himself from them, opens up as if automatically and is ready to change and to accept the norms sedimented in the life-world not only as external but also as inner determinations. Looking back on Hegel's determination of "absolute morality" as the unity of freedom and necessity, this now means that, if the domain of freedom built itself up on the path to a fulfilled belonging on the basis of community as the result of this generalizing and interiorizing path, its coercive character, that is, necessity, would disappear. At the end of the path the possibility would exist of a life oriented by com-passion based on the virtues of social justice and social sympathy, pervaded by the force of the capacity for com-passion as the *measure* that has settled in the individual in such a transformative way that he would act in accordance with it self-evidently.

III

In which organized form of a life-world would the life-world comportment which has become socially just and compassionate on the path described above, be most capable of acting *freely* in a manner appropriate to itself? What would the organizational forms of a society, in particular its state form, have to look like, in order for a person who has become transformed into one acting according to social justice and feeling compassion to live in it freely? Let us emphasize at this point once more that we are inquiring into the possibilities of social configuration phenomenologically; we are proceeding in an expressly contrafactual manner and are not describing facts.

What is certain is that it would have to be a social body with enough room for the development of life, room for the individual to take part sympathetically in the fate of the whole of his society. No social structure is, as we have said, possible without *order*. Thus, there must be a basic law, a constitution. This and the corresponding legal order must be acknowledged as an order that grants every one, within the limits of the possible, a sphere of freedom with respect to that order and in which the individual is able to live in accordance with the measure of the capacity of compassion. This would be the content of the material belonging essentially proper to man.

But how, particularly, would a state-structured belonging to the life-world, have to be organized so as to guarantee the corresponding sphere of freedom, necessary for a life to be spent in accordance with the measure of the capacity for com-passion? If we orient ourselves to the circumstances in the "Western world" in order to answer this question, this is only as an example. Whatever their particular structure may be, if a member of an order constituted by a state is to actually or (as is unavoidable in large states) "fictively" recognize himself within it the free election of representatives of a legislative House of Representatives—and thus a democratic order—would be required. If this order were, in addition, "liberal" in the sense that is connected with this term in Western constitutions, then the coercive character of the organizational structure would be alleviated as far as possible. In this lies also the requirement that there be fundamental rights guaranteed by a constitution to every individual as a legal person. Likewise, society must be secured as a constitutional state. Without these there can be no security under the law, which guarantees protection against every breach of the law that holds for everyone, and which is precisely its universal character. The fundamental norms of a constitutional, liberal state with a democratic constitution would have to guarantee unity and order and would have to enable every one to assume and maintain this membership in joint responsibility and his social virtue in the appropriate attunement.

A *welfare state,* for example, would satisfy the essence of man, his sociality, discussed in this inquiry. It would create the external condition necessary for the determining force of the capacity for com-passion to exert its influence in the social realm. This sympathy should not, however, call the liberal, constitutional, and democratic character of the state order into question. This state should be equal to the tasks of a constitutional state: by means of an absolutely binding legal order, which guarantees security under the law, it would have to defend the individual against arbitrariness and violence above all, and against the offense of injustice in its different forms as it is defined by a penal code. In all, it would have to protect each and every one in the same manner through a common legal system, acknowledging her as a legal person. In such an application of the "principle of equality" together with the principle of freedom, the objective side of what we designated as the material a priori of belonging reveals itself; the form of the state is shown that seeks to protect, or to alleviate the suffering of its citizens on the basis of a concrete constitution that provides unity and order, as a welfare state.

In this "objectified" form of subjective mentality, it becomes even clearer what the capacity for com-passion in the element of sociality means and what it does not mean. It does not mean the attunement and the immediately rational insight into the fundamental mode of man's being on the basis of which the individual is able to experience the other as a fellow-man in such a way that he no longer makes a distinction between his suffering and that of the other, for the latter, just as he himself, is subjected to the fate of mortality and the transience of life. This force of the capacity for com-passion, which develops the virtues of the relations borne by an individual to another, is played out in the experience or nearness. Nearness, however, is not "divisible." And yet all Dasein also exists as the potential of the social capacity for com-passion that can be developed into social commitment. If one wants to determine the content of this commitment, one should orient oneself towards its tasks, which we recognized as those of a welfare state. Can a person without a model to emulate, become wholly conscious of her membership and assume in a transformative way the fundamental bearing of her social essence? The immediate models should be the civil servants forming the executive in a state, as well as those of the judiciary and members of the legislative power, who, in the fulfilling of the duties entrusted to them in a liberal welfare state, are imprinted with the measure of the capacity for com-passion as a self-evident mentality. Admittedly, these are only demands, though they issue from the essence of man's sociality. These considerations are valid for our question even if the determinations gained from them can only be described contrafactually in today's world.

Man can "awaken" to his sociality just as to his essence of being a mortal, because both are not an alien, abstract capacity but rather that which is most proper to him, and because they both issue from the same source—the capacity for com-passion, even if they do so in two different respects. It is a phenomenon that time and again withdraws from our view and which the phenomenologist can, and must, render visible.

The preceding observations have already shown that the life that experiences meaning is not realized in isolation, but is always already related to a life-world which is given beforehand—indeed this life can only fulfill itself "in" the life-world. Precisely this traces out the path of our further analyses. In these it will be a question of determining this mode of being related, particularly as it regards the relation to the world on the part of the ethical attitude based on the capacity for com-passion.

What is the relation between the life that experiences meaning and the world? Just as in our life we are oriented towards the meanings of being-with our fellow-men, we also direct ourselves towards the world and worldly connections of meaning. Life experiencing meaning and the world belong together, and in such a manner that this belonging together is not a whole formed out of the sum of its parts. The philosophical tradition proceeded from the assumption of an all-encompassing whole but then tore it asunder in distinguishing between a "subjective" and an "objective" side. Admittedly, Descartes, who taught this separation of the *res cogitans*, the subject, from the *res extensa*, the object, the world conceived as extended, wanted to overcome this severance by the reverence back to God who, being *one*, unites essence and existence. Also after Descartes the "Idealist" philosophy beginning with Kant sought again and again to close the gap between subjectivity and objectivity on the ground of a "philosophy of consciousness." Thus, Hegel ultimately conceived of a subjectivity that encompasses its objectivity.

Contemporary philosophy attempts to overcome the split between subject and object by "stepping beneath" it. Thus, Husserl conceived consciousness as "intentional" and as constituting "objective" themata in its noetic acts; directing itself intentionally towards things and the world, it seizes its *intentum,* its *noema,* and thus constitutes an original order. Heidegger thought the structures of being-in-the-world in *Being and Time* in such a way that, it made accessible to Dasein interpreting itself an occurrence lying ahead of the split between subject and object. The later Heidegger turned around this being-in-the-world and conceived world as being originarily accessible in experience to a "turned" thinking.

In the previous chapters, we attempted to ground our *first thesis*. We showed how man, in his life that experiences meaning, in the element of attunement and through an intuitively rational seeing and hearing, can be shaken out of the everyday indifference of his life-world and can attain an ethical attitude towards his fellow-men as well as towards social communities. With regard to the relation between *ethos* and the life-world, we must now pose the question: How is world given to the life that experiences meaning, and in which way does it "have" a world? How does "world" reveal itself simply in the indifferently attuned everyday of the life-world experience?

Life in everyday attunement as well as the philosophical tradition regard it as certain that the world is a "unity" or a "whole." Husserl and the early Heidegger still remain bound up with this tradition when they attempt to determine the world as a "unison of acceptance" or as a "totality of involvement" respectively. In contrast to this, we assert that it does not correspond to the essential character of the attuned life that experiences meaning to be related merely to *one* world. Thus, this is our *second* thesis, which has to be given a foundation in the following contributions: we can only do justice to the complexity of our relation to the world when we gain insight into the fact that there is a *plurality* of worlds corresponding to the respective attunements of the life that experiences meaning.

It is the intention of these observations to gain an answer to the question in which way the one who has been transformed "dwells" in the different forms of the measure that determine him insofar as the life that experiences meaning always corresponds with *many* worlds. Is there a relation to the world appropriate to the *ethos* of sympathy issuing from the capacity for com-passion and in what does it consist? And does not a life that has become aware of the plurality of meaningful connections demand such an *ethos*? Let us name then our *third* thesis: the ethical, the *ethos* issuing from the force of the capacity for com-passion, does not itself designate a world among the many worlds but rather presents something which pervades all worlds and contexts of meaning, being in this way like religion and art. It is not, however, something "identical" that perdures throughout all change but rather a force that permeates everything in the manner of a setting free. It settles atmospherically over all contexts of meaning, saturating them, as it were. In this sense, it is an effective power that is then capable after all of connecting the many worlds.

In order to explicate our last two theses, we shall investigate in the first of the following contributions, how and why the world, in philosophy, the beginnings of natural science, as well as in the indifferently attuned life that experiences meaning as such, with regard to its wholeness, unity, harmony, and order counts only as *one;* and we shall ask whether there is not rather a plurality of worlds. Furthermore, the question presents itself as to the kind of relation that these many worlds bear to each other. The second essay takes up this thread and examines how our life that understands meaning is formed in such a way that it is capable of dwelling in many worlds, both "at the same time" and "in succession." It ends with the question, which is significant for the matter at issue here, how the relation of ethics and religion to the many worlds is formed. The third essay concludes with the insight that the ethical, as it permeates the various worlds, is the unifying force and as such reveals itself as the measure that exists "on earth."

CHAPTER 4

Is There *One* World?

I

The fact that the world is to be thought as a unity or as a totality has always been undisputed by the philosophy that had an historical impact in the tradition. The matter of controversy has been whether it is a unity or a whole. It would be a unity if it were indivisible in at least one respect, not only factually but essentially—that is to say, necessarily. Alternatively, it would be a totality if it were necessarily made up of parts, if there were many separable "worlds." Unity excludes internal plurality, totality requires it.

This traditional conception that the world shows either the form of a unity or of a totality is always accompanied by the idea that it has an *order*. For being ordered lies as much in the indivisibility of a unity as it does in the fact that each part of a totality has its particular, unexchangeable position. Unity or totality of the world and their order determine each other reciprocally. The Greeks, who conceived the cosmos as being ordered by the *logos,* saw in this simultaneously that it necessarily had the form of a unity or of a totality. Conversely, this conception of a unity or of a totality of the world contained that of an order. For Orphic poetry, for Plato, for the Stoics, for Plotinus, the ordering *Logos* was the governing force and the cosmos accordingly had the form of the unity of an indivisible animated essence. For Ionic thinking, for Aristotle, and for the Epicureans, for whom *Logos* likewise guaranteed order, the world had the form of a whole constituted by parts. For the

Christians of late antiquity and for the Middle Ages the world, *mundus,* was ordered by the divine law, which implied that, as the "mirror of the one God" (Bonaventura), it had the form of a simple unity. Alternatively, because the *mundus* was conceived as being ordered hierarchically, it was thought of as a whole in which each part had its determinate position according to number or weight. In the modern period, the order of a mathematically determined, law-governed mechanics determined the world (Newton), and the unity conceived as *res extensa* (Descartes). Even for contemporary natural sciences the calculable order of the world contains at once the thought of its unity. For them the world "in itself" possesses from the point of view of the natural sciences the ratio of a mathematically designed spatiality, temporality, and causality, and to this corresponds rational-mathematical ordering thought. For the philosophy of the modern period (Kant) this ordering thinking of ratio takes the form of synthetic a priori judgment, which by means of the categories, is capable of ordering the chaotic manifold given to the senses, of "unifying it into an object" in such a way that empirical experience achieves general validity and necessity. For this experiencing the world has become "the comprehensive concept of a totality," which must be conceived as an "idea of reason"— which cannot be experienced—in addition to the appearances—which can be experienced in infinity. Not only for theoretical experience does the world becomes an idea of reason. For Kant considers it is also the "intelligible" domain for man's practical comportment, the "realm of ends in themselves" to which man belongs as a *noumenon,* as the being that can determine itself and set rational laws for itself, submitting itself to them in freedom, and thus being able of giving itself this form of "order." Whether it be in the theoretical domain—as a priori or empirically—or in practical comportment, the ordering principle for philosophy no longer lies in the world but rather in the activity of the "subject," be it pure, empirical, or practical, and the world is no longer an "in itself" whose form could be determined as the unity or the totality of a cosmos, *mundus,* or a *res extensa.*

When in the following period, human self-under-standing attributes the ordering power increasingly to the subject, and this power is restricted to in the realization of an empirically planning, calculating, and thus a merely "rational" comportment; when the world has become a cal-culable quantum for the natural sciences and has ceased to be in itself a unity or a totality for philosophy and to grant man unity or wholeness, then there arises a need for phi-losophy to seek a "more originary" order of human rela-tions and their world. Is there not an order in force that does not need to be grounded by the theory of the mathe-matically proceeding natural sciences or that would be inde-pendent from the moral law before practical comportment posits it as moral law? Does "world" not have a meaning that designates something other than the mathematical system of formulae accessible to only a few scientists today?

The philosophies of Life developed by Bergson and Dilthey, but particularly Edmund Husserl's phenomenol-ogy, have sought such a "more originary" order of a more originarily apprehended meaning of world. Whether this order is characterized as an "originarily conceived *logos*" or as a "pre-logical dimension," is unimportant. What matters is to see that these efforts must be appraised as a desperate attempt to seek a new order or a new concept of world. Granted, however, that the order of such a "natural concept of world" could be demonstrated (as Husserl tried to do, fol-lowed by Heidegger in *Being and Time*), would it be a fore-gone conclusion that this order as well would be matched by a world that is either a unity or a whole totality, as was considered necessary in traditional philosophy? Is *one* world the necessary correlate of this more originary order of a more originary meaning of world? Precisely this is the question of our inquiry.

II

Let us ask at first which meaning we connect with the expression "world" in our everyday life when we do not comport ourselves in a scientific and technical way but rather rely on "healthy common sense" in an unreflected way and in an indifferent attunement. Admittedly, an answer to this question requires reflection on such comportment, but it does not at first reflect on how the meaning of world comes into being for the natural everyday process of bestowing meaning.

Clearly, by world we always mean something *spatial* at first, a space in which we perceive or in which we become involved through our actions, a space which "environs" us as corporeal beings, a space in which things are found with which we live, the things of nature, landscapes, mountains, and seas, as well as the things manufactured by crafts and technology. It is the space in which we either deal with those things that are very near, which we perceive or transforming; or it is the space for all the things that are as yet far from us and with which we could become involved at some point. World is further connected with the meaning of a space in which we encounter all kinds bodies, bodies of animals, but above all bodies of beings with minds, which resemble us, of fellow-men. And here as well it is the space for both the beings near to us, which we encounter, and for all the possible beings that are far from us and that we could encounter at some point. World means this kind of space which has nothing to do with the sense of space conceived in the mathematical natural sciences. It is not a question of a calculable, infinite quantum.

The everyday meaning of world apprehended in an indifferent attunement is not only connected with this particular sense of space but also with the sense of a particular kind of *time*. World for us is that within which we can comport oneselves "now," "before," or "afterwards." This domain for our comportment now, beforehand, and afterwards is, however, not one that could be measured and fixed with a clock. Precisely with regard to this non-measurable time does world have the sense of a "temporal" space.

In the third place, world is connected for us with the sense of a dimension in which *changes* take place. Here it does not matter whether it is we who have occasioned the changes or whether they have taken place "from outside," say, because of the things "out there" or through other people. It is not merely a question of changes that can be measured by determinate changes of place, but any kind of changes, including those that we perceive in the sudden mood change of a fellow-man. When we say that this fellow-man has changed this could only be possible for us in the world, that is to say, within a dimension in which alone there can be changes.

Finally, we connect with the meaning of world that of a world *for everyone*. In doing so, of course, we think first of "everyone" as the fellow-men of the cultural community in which we live. But beyond this, world means for us a temporal space in which changes take place in the way we are with, and for, each other—with, and for, all the people who dwell on this planet. With this short characterization, we have by no means exhausted the meaning of world as we understand it in the everyday of our sallow attunement. Let us stop for a moment, however, and ask ourselves whether the world we have thus characterized and which has nothing to do with the world of formulae conceived by the mathematical natural sciences, possesses an order peculiar to itself. We already mentioned an aspect of order when we discussed the fact that we encounter things, bodies, and our fellow-men in the world in immediate nearness or at a distance. Nearness or remoteness are precisely not measurable in their essence and cannot be determined by mathematical or calculating judgment. In the appropriate attunement, a fellow-man can be very near to us, although he is many thousands of miles away and, conversely, someone can be remote from us while sitting opposite us. Likewise, the "above" and "below," the "right" and "left" as it is determined by the localization of our body represent an order that is also not a mathematically measurable stretch. The fact that we do not confuse left with right and that we can distinguish between nearness and remoteness, undoubtedly implies a certain way of being ordered and one of the kind on which we can rely. This means that it is *always* so for us, without connecting the sense of "eternity" to this "always." Temporally speaking as well, the world of our everyday meaning has an order inasmuch as we can assume with certainty that the "afterwards" will *always* be next, and never the "before" or the "now," hence that each thing possesses its determinate temporal position. Finally, even changes, like the change of a mood, are not without a certain determinateness. While it may be very difficult to establish all the "conditions" under which moods can shift, "rules" can be set up within certain limits and psychiatry has made precisely this its task in recent times.

These are only a few examples of the orders that appear in the world of everyday life. Now before we extend further the meaning of world as it is apprehended by the indifferently attuned everyday life, let us ask, with regard to the interest guiding these investigations, whether the idea of unity or totality is connected necessarily with this order of the world, as was the case for the tradition. Does this pre-logical order possess the logical sense of unity or totality?

We recall this logical sense: unity excludes internal plurality, thus a plurality of worlds, and requires indivisibility in at least one respect; totality entails plurality, parts or worlds. It seems to us that, on the basis of the characteristics we have mentioned, no unequivocal answer is possible. The fact that the world is a space in which things, bodies, and fellow-men are encountered does not say anything about whether it is indivisible in a certain aspect, and it says just as little about whether it is a whole consisting of parts or worlds. In our everyday understanding of the meaning of world, we really only assume that it "surrounds" us. Whether it is essentially indivisible or divisible, and thus constituted by a plurality of worlds, is insignificant for that spatiality that we characterized and whose order we briefly outlined. Likewise, the traditional criterion of indivisibility for unity and of divisibility for totality bears no weight for the temporality of which we spoke. The same is true of world as the temporal space in which "changes" of whatever sort take place. However, this much can be said: the meaning of world, that we have hitherto developed and the order peculiar to it, require reciprocally that the world at least form a *context* [*zusam-menhang*]. For without a context it would not be thinkable that we could distinguish at all between what is near to us and what is far, between what is above and below, left and right, between what happens before, now, and afterwards, and what changes from one mode into another one. Our question as to whether the world is *one* or a whole would have to be answered with a "no" with respect to the traditional meaning of these concepts, as well as to their meaning in the everyday indifferent attunement.

The sense of world which we have hitherto determined is only a formal one. It pertains to the "external framework" of what we mean by "world." Beyond this, however, we connect a certain content with this expression. We speak of "our world" as a field with a wealth of meaningful contents that issue from a distant origin, from a "history." "Our world" consists, say, of the mores into whose domain of validity we are born as members of our people. It comprises the deposits of cultural products and of the historical experiences of our community. The content of our world is our whole "tradition," and also encompasses precisely that which occurs today in terms of the formation of meaning, the heightening of meaning, the decay of meaning—in short, the history of meaning as such—as well as all that which counts as the future aims of the cultural community to which we belong and of humanity as such. All these contents form a stock of "what is accepted in its indubitable existence,"[1] and to which we have immediate access through our mother tongue.

We grow up into this ensemble as children and appropriate it unquestioningly at first, operating self-evidently with these familiar matters. Language addresses these to us and we respond to its "call" in one way or another. In rare cases we ourselves transform these contents of meaning that have come down to us in a creative manner.

Let us ask ourselves if a world, whose context is thus determined, reveals a "pre-logical" order. Indeed many of the meaningful contents are given to us in a certain typical form. We can rely on them without being able to say that they will remain like this and not otherwise for all "eternity." The mores, in the way they hold in each respective community, are present in an invariant, fully reliable manner just as the legal norms to which we are bound. As members of this cultural community, we comport ourselves in this manner and not otherwise. We proceed at once from sedimented cultural, for example, religious, contents in the certainty that we shall also find them again in the future. There are certain practices, certain habitualities of the whole community, which have become our own and those of our fellow-men, which we thus presuppose as being self-evidently at work in them. To be sure, this or that cultural content of meaning may be transformed through historical events and cultural creations of meaning; in times of social or political revolution such transformations are indeed even predominant, and in the course of every life the meaningful contents on which communal life is built, change more or less radically. Yet by and large one can rely on the fact that they at least remain or change in a uniform way for the members of this community.

We now come to the most important question for our investigation. Does this order of the meaningful contents which thus determine the content of the world imply that it is a unity or a totality in the traditional sense? Is there, in the perspective of this pre-logical concept of world and its order *one* world or a *whole* world? An answer to this question may perhaps be found if we pay close attention to, and attempt to describe, the way in which we actually comport ourselves towards the world in the indifferent attunement of everyday life as the field of meaningful contents we have just characterized,—that is, if we comport ourselves towards it as an indivisible field of meaning, and thus as a unity, or whether we are always only involved in particular fields of meaning. Here it would be necessary to ask if these fields of meaning possess a structure of such a kind that they could count as parts of a whole. If an analysis of the way in which we comport ourselves towards the world reveals neither the structure of a unity nor that of a totality, then a new task poses itself, namely to determine the pre-logical structure in its pre-logical order.

III

Let us consider how we move in the midst of meaningful contents in our everyday comportment. For example, we act in the meaningful content of our professional life. The meaning of our profession consists of particular purposes and aims. In our professional comportment we are directed explicitly towards them, we submit ourselves to them self-evidently, and operate with them. As people engaged in a profession, we are at the same time determined by the meaningful content that issues from the fact that we are members of a family. We pursue our professions, for example, as fathers or sons. And as professionals and members of a family we are also members of our people, whose language we speak, into whose customs we are born, whose laws determine us as citizens, and whose politics and historical development have already steered us in one or the other direction in our decisions. Inasmuch as we are determined by the three contexts of meaning we have adduced as examples, we always play certain "roles." Most of these roles are unavoidable. We are born as members of a family, and even if we sought to escape from all familial duties, we still belong to the family despite our resistance to it. Likewise, we are born as members of a certain people and whether we want to or not, we take over its morals and its laws through our mother tongue. If we would separate ourselves from this people spatially, by emigrating, for example, or if we should reject its laws as anarchists, we still belong in one way or the other to its particular meaningful contents for the duration of our life. Similarly almost all people have some kind of job that determines them in one way or another in the practice of their lives.

Thus, the way in which we move within these meaningful contents is characterized by the fact that we cannot withdraw from them even if we wanted to. One can speak here of the *facticity* formed by the circumstances of our lives. It becomes still clearer when we call to mind the course of our everyday life more precisely. Already by going to work we must obey the context of reference represented by traffic system—car, train, streets. In our office we submit ourselves to the meaningful context of a communication system. These and many other contexts of meaning, above all those founded in technology, have caught us as in nets; we could not extricate ourselves from them even if we wanted to.

This insight into the facticity of our living circumstances is only significant for the answer to our question insofar as it makes clear that we *have to* relate to a plurality of contexts of meaning at the same time. This, surely, presents decisive evidence of the fact that we do not relate to *the* world as a single field of meaning, and hence that the world cannot have the form of a unity for us.

This provisional result would above all be confirmed by showing that we do not always only *have to* move in a plurality of contexts of meaning at the same time but rather that we are also *capable* of doing so. A reflection on this capacity would perhaps also shed light on the question of whether the manner in which we are always capable of moving in many contexts of meaning at the same time speaks to the fact that we relate to these as parts of a whole or whether we are dealing with a completely different and new structure in the form of this pre-logically conceived world.

We remain with the example we have chosen for a plurality of contexts of meaning and assume that we are involved in them at the same time. Who is this "we" or this "I" capable of doing this, and what are the conditions of the possibility of such a "directing oneself towards?" If we ask in this way, we give rise to the impression that we wanted to proceed in a traditional transcendental manner, framing our inquiry in a Kantian transcendental fashion. For Kant, however, the *logos* as judgment (be it a priori or empirical) was the starting point for the foundation of an order, whereas for us it is precisely the prelogical order of the

world that forms the basis from which we proceed. Hence,
it is out of the question from the very outset to see in Kant's
transcendental apperception, which unifies the manifold
given to the senses into an object, the condition of the possibility of the capacity for the Ego to direct itself simultaneously to a variety of fields of meaning. Nor do we inquire
into the condition of the possibility of a "pure" ego, but
rather into those of the capacity of a factual ego attuned in
such a way, which is capable of maintaining itself as identical throughout all change on the basis of its particular
habitualities. This ego, though factually always interwoven
with its experiences, possesses free activity and spontaneity. Through these it realizes this "directing itself towards"
many contexts of meaning. How can this manner of execu-
tion be characterized more exactly?

Already in traditional philosophy it was "attention"
(Hegel) that explained an active "directing oneself towards"
as such. Attention is frequently compared with an "illuminating light" and its object designated as that which is sit-
uated in a beam of light (Husserl). Now the illuminating
light can shine more or less intensely, the many fields of
meaning will accordingly be more or less strongly present
in the beam of light. Put differently, according to the individual degree in which one turns to the different fields of
meaning, it can be explained in which way and how
strongly the different modes of being conscious of something are present. They will be either topical actually or
less topical actually or only peripherally present. If we
speak here of being present, this contains an indication
that attention or turning towards something can ultimately be founded in turn in a particular kind of temporality as the conditions of the possibility of the capacity to
be in many fields of meaning simultaneously. It will be
temporality that ultimately provides a foundation for how
the topically present consciousness of fields of meaning is
synthesized with the less topical and the merely peripheral
ones. This process of synthesizing, however—and this must
be clearly marked—is only a question of the formal unifying of different fields of meaning, of "worlds," and not of the

constitution of the unity or a world synthesis through temporality. It is the condition of the possibility of our ability to be in many fields of meaning at the same time. However, the actual copresence in terms of content, given by the fact that when we, for example, direct ourselves towards the purposes and aims of our professional world, we do this simultaneously as members of a family and as citizens will be completely left out of this discussion of time.

A possibility of providing a foundation for this copresence in terms of content could perhaps be given in the concept of association. In carrying out our professional activities, we feel reminded simultaneously of the fact that we are members of a family because we are engaged in a job in order to provide for our family; likewise, we feel reminded of the fact that we are citizens by the fact that in pursuing our profession we take note of political events and do not infringe on laws. In any case, the concept of association indicates to us that it is necessary to pay attention as well to the "objective side," that is, the content of the fields of meaning and of the world itself, if we are seeking the conditions of the possibility for being able to direct ourselves towards many contexts of meaning at the same time. If we pay close attention to this, it is revealed that the impulse for this "directing towards" does not issue from turning the ego towards something or from attention but rather from the fact that fields of meaning affect us, stimulate us, announce themselves on their own. Clearly, while we are engaged in a profession, the most diverse references of meaning announce themselves as if of their own accord. We have to follow them if we wish to meet the claims of our profession in its aims and purposes. This announcing is the decisive step, and it alone can provide the starting point from which attention and interest are awakened.

But how is an announcing of this kind possible? How do these contexts announce themselves in different degrees of strength, and in such a way that the topical contexts are present together with the less topical and the peripheral ones? An answer to these questions lies perhaps in the fact that we always already *dwell* in all these contexts of meaning precisely because we are always already born into them. Thus, it is by no means the case that a group of new contexts of meaning are constituted; rather the potential ones with which we are already familiar are actualized in differing degrees of strength. The fact that more or less topical and peripheral contexts of meaning can be actualized "together" in this fashion presupposes that a connection exists between them. It can easily be seen that the states of affairs, named in our example, that is profession, family, and people, belong together in one *praxis of life* and the praxis of life forms the context which, for its part, is always already there and which makes possible the co-presence of the many different fields of meaning when an actualization occurs.

For our problematic, it is important to emphasize at this point that this structure of a context that emerges from the praxis of life, can at once be made evident for the view of everyone. In contrast to this, nothing has hitherto been revealed that would speak for the fact that the different fields of meaning are parts that can be joined together into a totality that encompasses them, where this totality would be *the* world.

That the world does not possess the form of such a totality becomes particularly clear when we remind ourselves that we, after all, are not only capable of dwelling simultaneously in many homogeneous contexts of meaning, such as emerge from the *praxis of life,* but also in many heterogeneous contexts of meaning. One can think of the contexts of meaning instituted by our imagination, for example, those of play in general or of the theater in particular. Thus, we are immediately capable of stepping out of the sober everyday worlds into the magic world of a theatrical performance and of letting ourselves be captured by it, while we continue to belong to the fields of meaning of, for example, the world of the family or the world of politics. Although we live all day one in the sober contexts of, say, the world of our profession, we can simultaneously belong, as

religious humans, to the context of meaning issuing from
the dogmas of our religion. Here there is a coexistence of
fields of meaning, which precisely do not already in themselves belong to one context because they belong to one uniform praxis of life. Thus, one can discover here no context
that is potentially already present to hand and that would
then be actualized in a greater or lesser degree of strength.
Nor can the phenomena of attention, of turning towards
something and of temporality, adequately be shown to be
conditions for the possibility of our being able to direct ourselves towards these different contexts of meaning at the
same time. We can really only say that it is the decisive basic feature of these determinate worlds—such as dreams,
art, and religion—that they capture us as it were, that
they overcome us, that they are there without us, for our
part, being able to do much more for their presence than
being "open" to them. Admittedly, this is not a sufficient
"explanation" for the strange phenomenon that we live in
the everyday contexts of meaning, simultaneously and are
claimed at the same time by non-everyday contexts of
meaning. The decisive insight, however, is that these heterogeneous worlds are not even held together by a potential
context. On the contrary, they contradict each other essentially. Hence, it is out of the question to speak of *the* world
as a totality to which all "worlds," including the heterogeneous ones, after all must belong as parts.

IV

For traditional logical thinking, the concept of plurality includes the one of unity just as, conversely, the concept
of unity includes that of plurality. According to their meaning, both belong together inextricably, even when each of
these concepts is "posited" independently. These logical
concepts of plurality and unity have also entered into our
language in such a way that language almost forces us to
presuppose unity whenever we speak of plurality, and vice
versa. The same holds for the relation of the whole and its

parts. The concept of a part likewise includes that of the whole just as, conversely, that of the whole includes that of parts. This logical connection has also entered into language and forces us to think in this way.

Yet in our attempt to understand the fact that we dwell in many contexts we have come upon a plurality that belongs neither to a unity nor to a totality. We decide not to let ourselves be directed at once by the power of language but rather to be ready also to think "against" language. Let us stick to what is clear to us in evidence and let us not be tempted into postulating a unity or a totality because this would somehow "lie in the necessity of the concept" as it issues from our everyday, indifferently attuned attitude.

The contemporary state of the world has often been characterized as one of fragmentation or of alienation. This fragmentation and alienation has been perceived precisely in the fact that there is no longer *one* world or a *whole* world, which always also means the "hale" world. Thus, one pines in longing for a time in which this hale world still existed, for a "re-enchantment" of the world, or one attempts to restore it through Utopian designs of a usually political nature.

It might be precisely the task of philosophy, which has realized that there is no such unity or wholeness of the world, to free humankind from this barren longing. Man's highest dignity may lie precisely in the fact that he is capable of dwelling in many contexts of meaning at the same time, that he can take each individual context of meaning as such into account and appreciate it in its peculiar properties, without always having to incorporate it further in thought into a unity or a totality. Especially today it seems to be of the greatest significance to devote oneself to this task. While belonging to many worlds, to many different contexts of meaning, we who live on this planet dwell in ever greater proximity to each other. Each one of us must learn to allow the many contexts as such, to allow each particular one in its peculiar essence, to be as it is; one must learn to respect them and not lose oneself in the fruitless attempt to construct the manifold contexts of meaning into

unity or a totality. In the same manner, the issue every-
where else is to let each individual context of meaning be in
its peculiar properties, to dwell with it, to understanding it
ever more deeply. The relation in which we dwell as human
beings is not that of the concept, of the connection in which
what is other is the other of the one. It is rather the relation issuing either from the context of our *praxis of life* or
even without any connection, that encourages us to live in
many worlds at once.

We have spoken of the coexistence of the fields of
meaning of everyday worlds, which are integrated into a
context because they belong to a uniform praxis of life.
However, we have said that it is a context that can be actualized to a greater or lesser degree. We have said of the worlds
other than the everyday worlds that they overwhelm us in
each particular case, and that we can be *open* to their presence as the particular case arises. We have shown that
what is at issue here could not be a "totality," which in any
case cannot provide a sufficient explanation for the strange
phenomenon that we can dwell in many everyday and non-
everyday contexts of meaning at the same time.

Thus, if we cannot speak of a totality of many worlds,
the question still presents itself as to whether a force does
not exist that pervades the many worlds, which, however,
can hold them together as an atmosphere and permeate
them only if we do not dwell in our everyday world indifferently. We have already pointed out that in the case of the
dogmas of a religion it is not a question of a context that is
founded by a uniform praxis of life. At this point we pose
the further question: is there not also an ethical force beside the religious one, which is capable of coloring all the
life-worlds and of bringing them together into a "unity" in
this sense? Can it be shown that the capacity for com-passion
is such a force, which is experienced in an attunement accompanied by "seeing" and simultaneously "hearing" reason,
and which is capable of becoming effective in the heterogeneous worlds, even though in different ways. To be sure,
what is at issue here is not the unifying power of the con-

cept, not that of association, not the unifying faculty of attention, nor of the unity of a praxis of life. The following essays will show in more detail that, and how, the capacity of com-passion can become effective in the manifold worlds as an ethical, and as such unifying, force.

CHAPTER 5

The Life-Worlds in Their Plurality
and in Their Ethical Relation

When we pose the philosophical question about the world in what follows, we are not asking about the world as the whole of what is. We inquire rather about the way in which our comportment understanding meaning addresses itself to the manifold contexts of meaning which, since the eighteenth and nineteenth centuries, have been called "worlds," and to those worlds in the first place that, in our cultural sphere, belong to everyday human life: the professional world, the family world, the sociopolitical world, as well as the many contexts of meaning without which there would no longer be everyday life today, the worlds of transport and communication. In addition to this, we ask how the non-everyday worlds such as those of religion, ethics, and art present themselves in our comportment understanding meaning, particularly when it also moves in everyday worlds.

I

As far as what follows is concerned, we assume that there are contexts of meaning and that the fact of our comporting ourselves towards them in a way in which we understand meaning is philosophically relevant. In contrast to this, the tradition is concerned only with the question of a context that envelops whole and all that is how there is, is in this sense, *one* world. Thus, the Greeks asked how the *logos* unified all that is into a beautiful structure, the cosmos; the scholastics asked about a creation fashioned by the *deus creator* in the form of a unity, the *mundus;* Descartes posed the question as to the unifying principle of extension, the *res extensa,* which he called "nature"; Kant inquired into the "comprehensive concept of appearances" as "systematic unity"; for Hegel the question about the world concerned the unity of the form of objectivity taken by the one, absolute Spirit in which the world is grounded. When facing the question as to the comportment experiencing meaning with respect to this one world, which is conceived as a whole or as a unity, the philosophical tradition has mostly thought these determinations in terms of entities within the world; additionally, it has asked how a world thought in this way exists for knowledge and not for other forms of experience.

In a time in which the increasing rationalization through modern technology is bringing forth contexts of meaning that are ever less transparent to the layperson, and in which the social and political worlds, which are in constant transition, confront us with ever new meanings that always require different forms of comportment of us, philosophy must clarify that, and how, it is actually possible that our understanding of meaning is capable of relating to a plurality of contexts of meaning, of everyday worlds. Instead of complaining about the fragmentation of our relation to the world today, saying, for instance, that we can no longer cope with the plurality of everyday worlds, we must, first of all, stop and be amazed by the fact that our comportment understanding meaning apparently moves with ease and as a matter of course in many everyday worlds simultaneously and consecutively and that, in doing so, it is in no way confronted with chaos but rather that an order seems to be maintained throughout.

Philosophy can take up these questions because, unlike social or economic analyses, it carries through a reflection on the basic structure of human comportment in general. In this inquiry, we direct ourselves to the basic structure of the comportment that understands meaning. We no longer designate this comportment, following the

philosophical tradition, simply as "understanding" but
rather speak of the understanding of *meaning*. In doing so,
the expression "meaning" intends only to point to what every person means when he says of a certain matter, "It has
meaning," or "It is not meaningless." It is Only that which
we take to have some sort of "meaning" from the very outset however vaguely, can we form judgments upon and
draw conclusions from; only what has meaning do we attempt to define and to comprehend, to "understand" expressly, in the traditional sense of these philosophical
determinations. Thus, understanding meaning pertains to
a more originary stratum of Being than that which concerns understanding conceived in the traditional sense.
Speaking of understanding meaning in this way indicates
further that here something is intended, that this understanding is after meaning, hence, that it has meaningful
states of affairs or contexts of meaning as objects. Edmund
Husserl has shown that in the case of understanding meaning the issue is that what we encounter reveals itself to our
"intentional consciousness" within a horizon of precedant
significance. This precedant significance can consist of either a state of affairs interpreted in advance or in a context
of motivation oriented towards action, which can be articulated in language and which can thus possess a context
that is accessible to interpretation and that constitutes a
meaning. The everyday worlds as well as the non-everyday
worlds count as such contexts of meaning.

When in the following exposition we designate the basic structure at issue not only as "the understanding of
meaning" but often also as a *comportment* understanding
meaning, we do this to indicate that understanding meaning is not a question only of the fruit of a theoretical relation but rather of the product of an active orientation.

Precisely because of this active character in understanding meaning, it is important from the very beginning
to pay attention to the fact that, and the way in which, all
understanding of meaning is accompanied by an *attunement,* that is by the "mood" one is in. This is not the place
to discuss in general the role played by our "disposition,"

our "affecticity," in all the manifestations of our rationality. It suffices to point out that our comportment understanding meaning, accompanying all understanding comportment, "attunes" itself to the intended contents of meaning. The issue for this comportment is to apprehend them emotionally. In the course of this it can occur that the intended meaning is wholly or partially displaced. It is no proof against this possibility of the withdrawal of meaning that man, particularly in times when he is influenced by his great successes in scientific understanding, proceeds upon the assumption that everything that exists is intelligible. For, in thinking in this fashion, he disregards precisely the fact that in his everyday forms of comportment even the meaning of his own being, and in particular that of his mortality, is so disguised that it mostly comes into view only through the fright precipitated by an experience and through a radical attunement, like the horror felt by the one who encounters his continual "dying" for the first time as a fact.

II

To illustrate our question about the possibility of the simultaneity and the succession of different everyday worlds for comportment understanding meaning, we choose the example of a factory owner, who throughout the day has eyes and ears only for the particular purposes and aims of the determinate world of his profession. Thus would seem to be the case, yet we observe that precisely in carrying out his work, in being occupied with the problem of manufacturing and distributing his product, he submits himself to the frames of reference of wholly different worlds. He makes telephone calls and thus orients himself in accordance with the frame of reference of the world of communication. Without comprehending the complicated context of meaning of this system, he does all that is necessary for carrying out a telephone conversation. Furthermore, while he is directed intentionally towards the concerns of the world of interest pertaining to his factory, he does not lose sight of the political world of his country, nor of the particular laws and mores of the social world to which he belongs. And at the same time thoughts of his family world do not leave him, thoughts of whether, and how, the profits of his firm can benefit his family or of how he has to protect it from losses. These examples illustrate how, in moving within the relations of a particular world of work, one is related simultaneously to a multiplicity of other everyday worlds. One is also related to them in succession. The factory owner, for example, returns to the world of his family after his office has closed, or he lives temporarily in a political world, say, if he takes part in a political meeting.

The *attention à la vie* served Henri Bergson as an explanatory principle for the fact that in our conscious, waking, active life we hold now this, now that state of affairs to be "relevant"[1] and thus bestow our active interest upon it. In a similar way, Hegel has already regarded "attention" as one of the faculties of the subjective, spontaneous Spirit that grounds the sphere of the objective structure of objects in general, and which is thus one of the preconditions for the apprehension of a particular object; he conceives attention as a ray of light through whose illuminatory power an object can come forth as an object.

Is this insight into the operations of the *attention à la vie* and attention sufficient for a comprehensive explanation of the possibility of comportment understanding meaning that we clarified in the example of the factory owner? In no way does it explain the occasions in which he comports himself understanding meaning in different worlds at the same time. For is it not precisely the case that he lifts the receiver and follows the references that constitute the telephone system without for a moment paying attention to the world of communication as such, without being aware of it spontaneously? Or if, while carrying out his particular professional tasks, he also takes the political world into account and keeps an eye on the laws and mores of his social world, then surely this takes place because the contexts of meaning of the political and the social worlds "force themselves upon" him, and precisely not on the basis of a spontaneous attention or of an *attention à la vie,* which would at first bring these contexts of meaning into view as objective or relevant.

Attention and *attention à la vie* could also not be adequate explanatory principles for the cases in which the factory owner crosses over from the professional world to that of society, of politics, or of the family, and in which he experiences them successively. For surely a decisive precondition for the understanding of meaning that is able to pay attention now to this world, now to that one, is the fact that the particular understanding of meaning in each case is carried out on the basis of a *context of meaning* that is maintained throughout all change; otherwise *one* respective act of paying attention to a context of meaning, a world, would be the end of understanding meaning as such and a *next* act of being attentive would be altogether out of the question.

In his own way, Kant already deduced in the *Critique of Pure Reason* that the consciousness of the ego—self-consciousness conceived as a transcendental logical function—constitutes a "qualitative unity" maintaining itself throughout all change. Edmund Husserl revealed phenomenologically that consciousness constitutes itself as the connection of *one* stream of experiences out of inner time-consciousness—that is to say, whenever it seizes the present, thus this present point in time, it experiences past events as a horizon within this present, consequently also holds on to what has just passed, so that an interpenetration takes place in which a continuity, the connection of consciousness, is constituted. Evidence of this or another kind for the possibility of a context of understanding meaning that is maintained throughout change, would in any case have to be added to the functions of attention and of *attention à la vie* if these are to explain why our understanding of meaning is able to move through many contexts of meaning successively.

Above all, attention and *attention à la vie* do not take the phenomenon into account that the understanding of meaning, which is able to relate to a plurality of everyday worlds successively, is nevertheless accompanied with the certainty that chaos does not rule, that there is rather a certain order of everyday life which does not only apply to this understanding of meaning but also to that of all the fellow-men in a cultural sphere.

Yet how are we to take the particular kind of order that holds for the everyday understanding of meaning that relates to a plurality of everyday worlds? How can it be explained that the everyday worlds are taken by us as ordered among themselves? An insight into this particular kind of order of the everyday worlds among themselves could lead to an answer to our question as to how our understanding of meaning can move in a plurality of everyday worlds simultaneously and successively.

III

It has been shown up to now that all understanding of meaning is directed to a meaning, and in the case we have before us, to a context of meaning. Let us now pay attention to this side of the context of meaning intended by the comportment understanding meaning, that is to its *intentum*, thus to the "objective side"—not losing sight of the fact, however, that each "objective" context of meaning only has meaning for a "subjective" intentional understanding of meaning directed towards it. At first we have to clarify the question as to whether each of the contexts of meaning, each everyday world, has the validity of an "inner order" for our understanding of meaning. It is only subsequent to this that we can ask if there is an order to the relation of the everyday worlds among themselves, and of what kind it is.

We have already seen that a particular professional world, for example that of a factory owner, has its particular aims and purposes. The factory owner is oriented to-

wards them and this being oriented of his "intentional consciousness" can be grasped using a phenomenologically
conceived determination in such a way that not only the
kind of inner order, which each of the everyday worlds possesses, but also the kind of order formed by the connection
of the everyday worlds comes into view. This determination
is that of the *theme*. We can say with regard to the factory
owner's particular professional world that it is the theme of
his comportment understanding meaning. But when, more
precisely, do we speak of a "theme?" When one asserts in
the form of an existential judgment: "This church is located
in this particular town," one has not "made it into a theme."
This would be the case if one were to discuss this fact historically, say, if one were to speak of the period in which
this town had been built against the background of the social and political conditions prevalent at that time. One
could also make this church into a theme by speaking about
its role in the cultural life of this town today, given contemporary social and political conditions. One could go far
afield here and come to speak of matters that only peripherally concern the theme. And then there are those matters
of which everybody knows that they no longer belong to the
theme, and are irrelevant to it. This reveals that the theme
contains within it its own "order." It is not tagged on to it
from the outside. Of course, depending on the approach,
one can treat the theme in one way or another, attributing
a significance to particular relations that they did not have
on the basis of a different attitude. Still, our understanding
of meaning with respect to a *theme* is bound principally to
an inner order, which it reveals "of its own accord." Our understanding of meaning cannot correspond to an order at
will or go beyond the limits of the field outlined by the
theme itself. One can clearly see once more that in this respect both *attention à la vie* and attention, conceived as
spontaneous comportment, represent completely inaccu-
rate explanatory principles from our perspective. Surely, it
is rather the case that the relations of order within the
theme itself force the factory owner's comportment understanding meaning to turn to these and not to those matters

within his professional world. They demand his interest. The markets of labor, goods, and consumers, which come into question for manufacture, the people active within this world and likewise determined by its contents of meaning, the things inasmuch as they have derived their meaning from this world—all of this prescribes the theme to the manufacturer, prescribes to him how he must comport himself thematically towards his professional world of work, understanding meaning.

What has been said up to now pertained only to the "inner order" of a respective context of meaning, of an everyday world that is the theme of a comportment understanding meaning. However, we are looking for an answer to our question as to how the fact can be explained that we live in the certainty that there is the order of a connection of the many everyday worlds. In doing so, we hope to receive with the answer to this question an answer to the problem that motivates us here, namely, how it is possible that we are able to move successively and simultaneously in these worlds? We ask: Have the single everyday worlds among themselves the validity of an order common to everything, binding for all those who belong to it? Hitherto we have referred to these worlds as everyday worlds. Instead of speaking of their everyday character, we could also say that it is a question of worlds that are necessary for the carrying out of the *praxis of life*. Could perhaps a reflection on the meaning of the praxis of life bring us nearer to the order we are looking for, and give us an answer to our question as to how the connection of the everyday worlds among each other for our understanding can be thought in a way that is valid for all these worlds?

The *praxis of life* has for us—unquestionably—the validity that is real. Precisely because of this we hold, conversely, that the world of art or of dreams is "unreal." Each of us knows immediately if the worlds we have hitherto designated as everyday belong to the praxis of life or not. Obviously, we take our professional world to be part of the praxis of life; the social world, with its institutions necessary for the realization and the maintenance of life, equally partakes of this character, and this is also true of the political world whose events affect our lives in different ways.

The world of our closest community, the world of the family, also has meaning as praxis of life. Likewise, we take the plurality of worlds that have been founded by technology to be a part of such a praxis without further ado. And for life today, a system of communication and of transportation seems to be altogether indispensable.

If we relate to the individual worlds as belonging to the *praxis of life*, the meaning of what constitutes this praxis must be known to us. Does this mean that the validity in terms of the praxis of life of each individual world, as well as the meaning of the praxis of life itself, form a theme of our comportment understanding meaning? Do we orient ourselves in everyday life towards this meaning in the same way as the factory owner does with regard to the aims and purposes of his factory? Or is it not rather the case that we are only vaguely aware of the fact that the worldly contexts of meaning mentioned hitherto pertain to the praxis of life? Are we not rather aware in an unthematic manner of the meaning of the praxis of life, on the basis of which we relate to it as life-practical, while we are engaged thematically with the aims and purposes of the professional world?

Indeed, the content of meaning of the praxis of life as such is rarely a theme for us in our everyday comportment. This is not contradicted by the fact that we can make it into a theme philosophically, and precisely in the manner in which it is valid unthematically for the understanding of meaning in everyday life. We can clarify this meaning, and its particular mode of being, in correspondence with which it is always already given to us as already known and in which we are familiar with it long beforehand.

Let us attempt to clarify the meaning of the praxis of life in what follows because we indeed suspect that a particular type of connection is founded in this general meaning of the praxis of life, precisely inasmuch as it is not an explicit theme, and that we can find in the order of this connection what regulates the relation of the individual everyday worlds among each other. In this we proceed from the assumption that insight into this order could lead to an answer to our question about our ability to relate to the plurality of everyday worlds both in simultaneity and in succession.

IV

At the beginning of these expositions we already mentioned that Greek philosophy saw the principle of the order of the world in the *logos,* in the logical that was later called the "rational" *logos,* which was the "beautiful structure," the "cosmos" for the Presocratics, was conceived at the same time and ever more clearly as the "thought" whose determinations specifically regulate man's thinking and the content of his thought. *Logos* was taken to be eternal and necessary. Since time immemorial the essence of the *logos* and of the rational also contained the fundamental characteristic that it granted total openness, in such a way namely that everything sensuous and affective was either conceived as negative and inconsequential or, as in Hegel's philosophy of Spirit at the end of our tradition, considered as "sublated" [*aufgehoben*] in the sense of *conservare* and *elevare.*

All this, then, also characterized the traditional philosophy of Reason and of Spirit and its methods, which inferred from or deduced towards a primary principle or proceeded on the path of dialectical presentation, which was embodied in its most complete form in Hegel. It was against Hegel, and thus against the claim to power on the part of *Logos* in general, that the Left-Hegelians Feuerbach and Karl Marx, and then Kierkegaard and Nietzsche, directed their thought. At the present time, philosophy of life and phenomenology have attempted to reveal relations which, being "more originary," lie at the base of traditional logic. They are not deduced according to the principle of reason but described as structures; they are no longer taken to be "eternal" and "necessary," but considered explicitly as "having come into being historically."

Thus, what in the preceding discussions was designated as an "inner order" of the individual everyday worlds and their respective "theme", was also described in this fashion as a structural context that has come into being historically. The structure of rules contained in the theme "modern factory" does not prescribe a mode of Being that has been valid from all eternity and necessarily to the factory owner's understanding of meaning, but rather one that has developed from the long history of his professional field.

Let us now characterize in greater detail this structure of a particular world in the respect that it is not only the thematic object for a factory owner but, as such, also possesses the meaning of the *praxis of life*. Here we employ a further determination developed by phenomenology, that of the *type*. The meaning of the praxis of life is a type. When we say, in a general sense that "something seems 'typical' " to us, or that "we act in a 'typical' manner," this expresses that we are familiar with the its mode of being of the typical in the matter at hand. The fact that I handle something in a typical fashion means that I do not first have to view it from all sides in its own right and reflect on its meaning for a long time. From childhood onwards, and solely, through the medium of the language into which we grow up and in which all typical meanings are sedimented, our understanding of meaning of the types of things, humans, animals, and indeed of everything that can be experienced in general, is predetermined. These are complex matters that have hitherto by no means been clarified, and it is not our task to discuss them in detail here. The same is true of the contexts of meaning in "structures," and thus also of the structures of our everyday worlds in which the praxis of our life runs its course, and which we therefore call the life-practical. Thus, we are immediately at home in the forms of realization of the systems of traffic and communication, and we comport ourselves towards them in typical ways because we encounter them as "types" despite the complexity of the systems on which they are based. We relate to the world of our family in its typical forms with the same confidence. Of course there are worlds whose meaningful structures of rules become familiar to us as typical only after a long period of learning and practice, thereby becoming "habitual." No one, for example, becomes a factory owner overnight. The understanding of meaning on the part of the factory owner has come forth from a multitude of different experiences concerned with the aims and purposes of a factory as their theme, which has been developed in such a way that he is familiar with the manifold structures of a professional world and considers them "typical." The type which they embody is that of the praxis of life. It belongs to the type "praxis of life"—and this is decisive for the answer to our question—that it is also experienced as being such by our comportment understanding meaning when it is not an explicit theme. The mode of being that belongs to the type of the praxis of life provides the explanation for the fact that our understanding of meaning is related to this type precisely in an unthematic way, having always already understood it. We always already dwell in the meaning of the praxis of life as a type and we apprehend each individual everyday world as belonging to the praxis of life on the basis of this type as a general meaning. The fact that we never really comport ourselves towards an everyday world as an "isolated" one is entailed by the generality of this content of meaning. This general meaning pervades all the everyday worlds that belong to the type of the praxis of life, and it connects each individual everyday world with all the other life-practical worlds. This explains our being able to be led without further ado from one everyday world, in the form stamped on it by the praxis of life, to another one.

In the history of the experiences that many generations of a particular cultural community have had with the general meaning of the praxis of life, typical furrows have come forth as paths leading from one life-practical world to another. In this historically developed way, the meaning that is common to everything does not only hold for me alone, but rather as a type—that is, as the general mode in which it directs the understanding of meaning of all the people belonging to a particular community and bestows the validity of an order onto everyday life and maintains it precisely through this. This order, however, is not one that could be conceived as a unity or a totality in the traditional sense, represented by the logical and systematic enclosure of a system that is based on, and grounded by, the principle of the *logos*. The general meaning of the praxis of life as a weave of relations is rather taken to be the order of a structural context that consists of an enduring unison of validity and that remains open to the entrance of new validities and thus to historical transformations.

An understanding of meaning that maintains itself unthematically though in typical familiarity in this general meaning of the praxis of life, in this type that interweaves the relations of the individual life-practical worlds among each other, is indeed related to meaning in such an "intimate" way that this relation can only be defined accurately as the *dwelling* of the understanding of meaning in this general meaning of the *praxis of life* and its connections.

On the basis of this insight into the way in which the comportment understanding meaning dwells in the relations that are in force within the various worlds, and in which the general meaning of the praxis of life leads one from one life-practical world to another, an answer can now be given to our question as to how it is conceivable that comportment understanding meaning is capable of being involved in a plurality of everyday worlds both simultaneously and successively. The fact that the factory owner, although seeming to move only within the horizon of interest prescribed by his theme, is nevertheless related to other worlds simultaneously or successively, is conceivable because he is also familiar unthematically with his particular world as a typically life-practical world, precisely on the basis of the horizon of the general meaning of the praxis of life as a type that is given to him in familiarity beforehand. Within the meaning of this type of praxis of life, the path is already outlined that leads in each individual case from one particular life-practical world—say, that of the factory—to other life-practical worlds in his community. The meaning of the *praxis of life* refers the understanding of meaning into the typical paths that belong to it, so that the understanding of meaning can, and indeed usually must, move, in the same living present, simultaneously within the concerns of the factory world, of the world of a more intimate community, of a social and political world.

At this point, we see clearly that, although these relations are only experienced unthematically as a horizon, they are effective without attention first being directed towards it spontaneously or an *attention à la vie* first having to bring one or the other particular everyday world into view for the understanding of meaning as being relevant or objective. The converse is rather the case. The factory owner is precisely required to also take the typical relations to other worlds into account precisely because the meaning of the praxis of life refers him to them. The political and social world "announces itself" as if of its own accord and forces the factory owner to turn to it because the factory world, as one belonging to the praxis of life, would not be capable of existing without regarding the laws and customs of the country or without the institutions of the city that provide for the factory. It is only because the factory owner's understanding of meaning always already "dwells" in the life-practical relations formed by the worlds among themselves, that he is "recalled" from one life-practical world to the other, and that he moves in them simultaneously, to a certain degree through association.

Following what has been said, it will be evident at once that precisely the basic structure formed by the understanding of meaning—which always already dwells in the weave of relations of the worlds among themselves, given typically in outline—that precisely this context, this "order," is also the condition of the possibility of the fact that we can also move successively from one particular world, for example, the professional world, and enter into another one, say that of the family or of the political world, and that we are able to move within them.

To avert misunderstanding, we further note that the fact that comportment understanding meaning submits both to the directions of the inner order of a particular everyday world and to the connection of the relations of the worlds among themselves, does not mean that such submission takes place "automatically" and without spontaneity. Both the thematic and the unthematic comportment towards the structures of rules of a respective world, as well as the unthematic comportment towards the typical relations of the worlds among themselves, requires an activity through which first an openness for these meanings is attained. Beyond this, an active integrating of these meanings takes place. To be sure, the determining factors for the majority of people are probably the already existing inner order, as well as the unison of validities of a particular individual world and the typical life-practical relations of the worlds among themselves. The fact that the plurality of worlds is often endangered against the wishes and the will of the individual by the monopolizing tendency of a dominant conception of rationality, like the rationality of means and ends of the technological and economic worlds, and the fact that it is very difficult to oppose the respective dominant priorities, let alone transform them— all this bears witness to the way in which the inner order of worlds imprisons us, as if with nets, thematically and unthematically and how we are caught in the particular relations of the "praxis of life"-type. Nevertheless, there is a leeway of possibilities within their orders, there, for example, where the inner order or the relations of the worlds among themselves could be improved by a greater knowledge of the matters at issue.

V

We conclude this exposition, with some considerations pertaining to the non-everyday domain. The religious and the ethical in particular count as non-everyday. Both are "forms of meaning" to which we relate as "understanding meaning." They are, however, neither isolated domains nor such that could be isolated; they are not worlds. The dogmas of religions claim to give the whole of Being its meaning. For the Judeo-Christian religion this whole is the creation of a creator God, a world that He has sanctified. The ethical claims to permeate each of the everyday worlds with its demands and thus to giving them meaning as a whole or a unity in this respect. Everyday worlds like the family world, particular professional worlds, and the social world are indebted to the religious and the ethical for the fact that the question of "meaning" is occasionally posed in them. For with regard to the everyday worlds, it can indeed be said that it belongs to their structure not to let the meaning by which they are borne above all come forth as meaning.

Non-everyday worlds as isolatable forms of meaning to which comportment understanding meaning is directed are especially the worlds of art—verbal, plastic, and graphic—, the many worlds of science—the purely theoretical ones as well as the technical and practical ones, like most of the natural sciences and medicine—, but also the worlds of theology and philosophy. In these, as in the everyday worlds, one would have to ask what makes up the unifying structure of each one and how it is possible that our understanding of meaning can relate simultaneously and successively to several non-everyday worlds. Above all the question arises here how it is conceivable that comportment understanding meaning, which moves in one of the several everyday worlds and thus in the overall meaning of the "praxis of life," can cross over into a non-everyday world simultaneously and successively. We shall start with this question in what follows.

Let us ask initially whether *attention à la vie* and "attention" would be sufficient as possibilities of explanation in this case. Let us ask this at first with reference to comportment understanding meaning that moves in the meaning of the praxis of life and turns in succession to the non-everyday world of art, in a case that we know well from in our comportment in the life-world, like a visit to the museum or the theater. The dominant view is that one should completely "eliminate" whatever pertains to the everyday and to the praxis of life in order to be able to actually engage in a non-everyday world. This is also expressed by the phrases that one should "abandon" all everyday matters and "plunge" into a completely different domain. It is quite accurate that taking in a work of art or a play requires us to turn away from the praxis of life and to turn to those contexts of meaning offered to us by such a work. Yet does not precisely what we have already become in each individual case play an important role for the possibility of adequately taking in the non-everyday meanings of a work of art or a play? One will surely not apprehend the work of art or the play, in a manner corresponding to its meaning until one has some life experience and a certain education, a certain experience in the domain of art. The meanings that already determine us before we visit the museum or the theater, be they of the life-practical sort or not, by no means disappear. They are rather the ones that must integrate these non-everyday worlds into themselves. The "crossing over" can be explained first of all by the structure of such a process of integration. Such integration should be conceived as a processing drawing in and not as a form-building unifying activity after the manner in which Kant conceived the "transcendental apperception," which gathers the manifold given to the senses by means of the unity of the concept into the unity of a conceptual object. Otherwise than in the philosophy of *logos,* here it is a matter of the gathering-into-itself of the non-everyday by the everyday, presupposing that the context of meaning of the work of art or the play is such that it allows itself to be integrated into the fulness of contexts of meaning, that constitute the high level of any given practical and "educated" history of experience. In distinction to the worlds of the praxis of life, which "announce" themselves to us, a considerably more active turning to the object is necessary in this "crossing over" to the non-everyday domain. Initiative is always required, which is motivated differently than in the life-world, in order for an exit from the praxis of life, which often, of course, holds us captive to a certain extent to take place. Initiative is needed for the visit to the theater or to the museum to be carried out at all. What is required here consists precisely

of motives that do not belong to the praxis of life, like a will
to learn and a questioning that is directed to education and
culture. In contrast to the life-practical worlds, there is no
direction for comportment understanding meaning does
not dispose of a reference, like the one given beforehand as
the connection of everyday worlds by the type of the overall
meaning of the praxis of life. Here there are no "furrows"
given to integration beforehand for the transition from
comportment understanding meaning in the praxis of life
to the non-everyday worlds of the museum or of the theater.
Within the framework of this investigation, we cannot go
into the question of why comportment understanding
meaning takes the trouble at all to cross over from a familiar world of the praxis of life to an "alien" world, like that
of the museum or the play, and to integrate itself into them.
We shall only say this much: We proceed from the assumption that comportment understanding meaning has a certain "sphere of freedom" and, without elucidating the
essence of freedom understood in this manner, it is sufficient here to recall the at least empirically demonstrable
fact that an active integration of the non-everyday world of
art is possible within the limits imposed on the comportment understanding meaning of a particular person for internal or external reasons. We indeed have the freedom to
enter into the full wealth of different non-everyday forms of
meaning in the world of art and to integrate them actively
into our everyday pursuit of life. Likewise, this freedom allows us over and over again to leave these and return to the
worlds of the praxis of life. The succession becomes a relation of understanding meaning that attunes itself increasingly to art, that indeed develops itself in such a way that
"crossing over" and integration becomes a matter of course.
Here the ease of returning can be explained by the fact that
the type of the overall meaning of the praxis of life has a
power of attraction whereas the entry into the non-
everyday world, the necessity of integration requires a certain "expenditure of effort."

To be sure, the necessity of making an effort in this
way can be very much greater in the case of entering scientific worlds. However, there are large differences here,

according to whether the one involved is an interested lay-
man or a researcher, who moves in his scientific world, ne-
gotiating it as a matter of course and thus being able to
exist in it and the world of the praxis of life almost simultaneously. For integration in this case becomes an increasingly "routine" matter. Being able to adapt oneself makes
the pains of integration almost disappear and thereby
hides the problem we have discussed here as a problem—
the question namely of how comportment understanding
meaning is able to effect this integration. An integration
that becomes a routine in this way and which, in terms of
its meaning, comes close to a relation of simultaneity between non-everyday and everyday comportment understanding meaning, is to be found in many scientific subworlds that are related to the praxis of life, above all in the
natural sciences and particularly in medicine.

But how does a theologian act, whose discipline does
not focus on the thematic object of a sub-world but rather,
as we have seen, on Creation as *one* world? Or one who is
ethically minded and who has appropriated the measure of
virtue for himself on the path we described? We have already said of the ethical force that it is also not a sub-world
but rather appertains in its demands to the whole of what
is. How should the simultaneity and the succession of comportment understanding meaning in relation to the everyday worlds be determined here?

We have already pointed out that the religious and the
ethical are capable of "permeating" all particular subworlds and above all the everyday ones. With regard to
understanding meaning itself this means that it does not
have to carry out the task of integration, which works new
contents of meaning into those which already fulfill the understanding of meaning. The understanding of meaning,
"permeation," is, on the subjective side, rather an intuitively rational insight in and listening to what happens to
it on the part of religious and ethical forces or what has always already happened to it—a process which is imprinted
essentially with the character of attunement and affectivity. The understanding of meaning in the everyday worlds

has always already received the contents of the religious world and the ethical force, or it finds itself in the midst of carrying out this reception, for permeation is a communicative process that never ends and that is never fully accomplished.

Still, the measure of the capacity for *com-passion* will bear different traits in the different worlds. In the world of the family, it will consist of the compassionate and loving care for members of the family. In the professional world say, of a judge, the capacity for com-passion will be at work in his interpretation and application of the law. Generally, it will reveal itself in relation to colleagues in the respective professions and, in the political world, it will have a role in influencing the political orientation in conjunction with other aspects. Depending on whether, and how, this permeation of the everyday worlds by the ethical and the religious as a communicative happening has taken place to a greater or lesser degree, our comportment towards these worlds bears a religious or ethical imprint, whether in the mode of simultaneity or in that of succession.

Looking back, let us ask what constitutes the philosophical significance of the present investigation. First, it has brought into view the ability of our comportment understanding meaning to orient itself simultaneously and successively towards many contents of meaning or worlds is not self-evident but rather points to a power that, measured against animal behavior, makes noticeable the riddle of human Being in respect that has mostly been neglected by anthropology. Second, we have indicated the tremendous wealth that lies in this possibility of calling to mind all possible contexts of meaning and worlds. In addition to this, the power of the religious and the ethical has become tangible, and the important role they play in our everyday worlds has been brought into view. In a certain sense they are always "also there" in our contexts of meaning, and whatever takes place in the many worlds depends on whether, and how, the measure of the capacity for compassion is effective within them. It is measure in this very particular sense in terms of which all comportment gauges itself. Thus, it is ultimately one and the same measure that reigns throughout the many worlds and which in this sense also unifies them. As far as the richness of the possible understanding of meaning is concerned, we have not spoken of all worlds in this investigation; we have not mentioned the worlds of play, of dreams, and above all of nature in the way in which it is always also there for our understanding of meaning in the form of mountains, forests, and lakes in spite of all industrialization. We have mentioned the fact that we can enter all these worlds, that we can leave them again, that we can cross over to an everyday world and then go from that one into a non-everyday world, and that we can experience these for ourselves simultaneously or successively. Looking back, we can perceive the significance of this investigation not only for the possibility of human "experience" but also for that of a human being's "being experienced." What would humans be without the possibility of the simultaneity and succession of worlds interwoven with the understanding of meaning, without the possibility of giving room to the religious and the ethical—possibilities which they have at their disposal and which they can develop or allow to wither away to a greater or lesser degree.

CHAPTER 6

The Richness of Our Relation to the World and the
Unifying Force of the Capacity for Com-passion

The question, "What really is *the* world in which we
can feel at home among the many contexts of meaning or
worlds?", unsettles the contemporaries, who cannot come
to terms with this plurality of contexts of meaning. Thus,
they create fantasy worlds, like that of the "good old days"
or of a "return to the roots" or of a new "immediateness," to
which they ascribe the most varied characteristics. This
can also be observed in serious endeavors in art and liter-
ature. There, too, one seeks original contexts of meaning,
for example, in those ancient civilizations that reached a
high level of development, like Egypt, Greece, Persia, or
China, or in the tribes of Africa and Australia, which have
had little contact with civilization. Similarly, certain move-
ments in contemporary philosophy are seeking an original
world. Once more there is a search for the "hale" historical
beginning of Western world history or the attempt in
thinking to prepare a new, different, "hale" beginning in
world history.

I

Particularly in the face of the fact that this one hale
world no longer exists, we should like to pose the question
if philosophy would not be well advised to focus on what it
can still find today, that is, the plurality of contexts of
meaning or of worlds within which human beings move
continually and simultaneously on the basis of the facticity

which we characterized (above). Perhaps now is the time to wonder at the richness made up by the fact that man can relate to this plurality and is able to determine the possibility of this relation philosophically. It is true that traditional ontology opposes such an attempt, having devalued plurality and alterity under the dominance of the *logos* as the unitary unifying force, inasmuch as for this ontology, plurality and alterity were only such with regard to the One. However, the question can be asked if contemporary philosophy, in so far as it no longer concedes exclusive dominance to the *logos* in several respects, could not liberate itself from this depreciatory view of plurality and alterity. To be sure, this is not possible as long as it seeks the One as "the root," and thus devalues plurality and alterity as being deficient.

The attempt at a philosophical determination of the facticity of human beings will have to proceed in such a way that, first of all, it thinks the plurality of worlds *as* plurality, and second, it conceives human life experiencing meaning in a fashion that takes this facticity into account.

An attempt to think plurality *as* plurality must endeavor to avert the temptation of allowing it to be transformed into a unity either by following the pull of the *logos* as thought and language, or by colluding with contemporary philosophy in singling out one of the many contexts of meaning as the only true and authentic one with respect to which all the others are deficient derivatives of the one source. However, the many contexts of meaning would possess no durability in their plurality, they would be "vanishing quantities" if they did not relate to each other. In the description of this facticity, we have already pointed out that a *transition* is possible between the contexts of meaning. Without the possibility of transition, man would not be capable of being in many contexts of meaning simultaneously. The fact of the possibility of transition would not exist if the many contents of meaning for their part did not bear a relation to one another. The question is, however, what kind of relation this is. It cannot be a relation of the sort conceived of by the "philosophy of identity." It cannot be a relation of "difference" that has issued from the meaning of unity or identity, and in whose meaning, in turn, there would be a reference to identity or to unity. Rather, it should be a relation whose meaning lies only in making possible a simple reciprocity of contents of meaning.

Let us attempt to determine this relation of contents of meaning to each other positively by proceeding empirically at first. The contents of meaning within the simultaneity of which man moves harmonize occasionally. But this is by no means always the case. On the contrary, one often moves out of the sober everyday world of practical necessity, the contexts of meaning of one's surrounding world, into a world of fantasy, play, or art, whose style is completely heterogeneous. This means that the relation that must be thought here, is as a relation that makes free transition possible and that is completely *indifferent* with regard to the content of the contexts of meaning. It is also indifferent to the different ways in which contexts of meaning relate to each other. They can relate to each other in a completely "neutral" manner (thus the context of meaning of the world of traffic within which I move in everyday life is neutral with respect to the world of my profession), or one context of meaning can determine the other. In time of war, the context of meaning of the political world determines the professional world and the world of the family. Contexts of meaning can also determine each other reciprocally. For someone living within the context of meaning of art, this context determines the world around him. But at the same time his environment determines, in a certain way, his conception of the artistic context of meaning.

Furthermore, the relation maintains the contexts of meaning in a certain "order," which remains largely "flexible." Because of this flexibility, one can bring into existence certain "hierarchies" within the plurality of contexts of meaning.

Finally, the relation is *open,* that is, it allows for the diminution, change, and increase of the plurality of contexts of meaning. Contexts of meaning die away while others appear for the first time or are brought into existence by individuals. Thus, a great artist initiates a new cultural period with new contexts of meaning. Political decisions and revolutions found completely new contexts of meaning.

Our empirical description allows us to designate, in summary, the relation built by the mutual reference of contexts of meaning in the transitional, indifferent, and open manner described above as *coexistence.* This coexistent relation of worlds to each other, however, does not exist "in itself," rather it only "is" because human life's modes of comportment experiencing meaning, as contents of meaning, are directed to it intentionally. Thus, the question presents itself as to how this life experiencing meaning itself, if it has to move in a *plurality* of contexts of meaning *simultaneously,* must be determined in its basic structure, in its "essence." This question can no longer be answered only empirically. Did the modern philosophy of consciousness already take that into account, for example, in that it no longer conceived what we called "life experiencing meaning" in a dogmatic manner as a substance as such but rather viewed it transcendentally as a nonsubstantial self and even as concept? To be sure, it held the self to be a "one." A "one" excludes plurality even if it is thought as a "side" that "faces" the other side, plurality or alterity. Hence, ways have to be conceived in which both these sides can come together and form an identity in order for experience, and knowledge in particular, to be possible. In the *Critique of Pure Reason,* Kant conceived this coming together of both sides as an "apperception" that gathers the plurality into the unity of the judging Ego, into this closed "one." For Hegel the Self, as the one side, is able to "pass over" to the other side and to "recognize" itself in it. In this recognition, he conceived the thought of the "return" as a "being-at-home-with-itself" of alterity.

The question must be posed as to whether the modern philosophical tradition has taken into account the facticity that has been demonstrated, which is the phenomenon that man always already has to move in many contexts of meaning at the same time. This is contradicted by the conception that thinks on principle in terms of "sides," and subsequently has to construct "connections" and "transitions." Kant, however, did see the phenomenon in its own right when he stated "The 'I' *must* be able to *accompany* all my representations" (emphasis added), and also inasmuch as he did not conceive the essence of man as substance. Yet he did not fully conceptualize that what is peculiar to the human self is that it "is" *at once* both with itself and with the other. It is precisely this that Hegel managed to do: he thought the Self as "concept." Precisely in this, the being of man rests in his completely unsubstantial "determination through Spirit." As subjective Spirit he is both an independent self and an "accompanying" being-with-the-other. Yet did not Hegel still leave this Janus-like double face of the self in the element of thought? Did he attempt to think it as *life* experiencing meaning? Precisely the fact that the "sublation" of all the basic forms of life into Spirit neglected the variety of human modes of life, was the object of several attacks, from the Left-Hegelians Feuerbach and Marx, through Kierkegaard to Nietzsche and the vitalistic philosophy of Bergson and Dilthey. Contemporary philosophers, Husserl and Heidegger in particular, have attempted to consider the life that experiences meaning. Husserl tried to determine the structures of the intentional flow of consciousness and the early Heidegger sought to bring the being-in-the-world of Dasein into view, both endeavoring to reveal these pre-logical spheres in such a way that they "stepped below" the dichotomy formed by the two sides discussed above. We cannot demonstrate here how Husserl, to be more exact, uncovered the "life" of the self precisely not as mundane and empirical but rather as transcendental in its intentional structures; equally, we cannot show how Heidegger brought Dasein in its facticity to intuitive evidence by means of a hermeneutic phenomenology directed against psychology and empiricism. The structures of the self conceived in this intentional manner as well as the existentialia of Dasein—and not only its basic modes that we have hitherto only taken up empirically—testify to the phenomenon that we are always already "with" the many contexts of meaning. Admittedly, we are completely at odds

with the later Heidegger's view, after the "turn," of the fact
that we "ourselves" are "in the company of" these contexts
of meaning. The self is, and remains, unique, irreplaceable,
and independent. Precisely because of this self-like character it remains as the same throughout all the changes of
time, as that which is also conscious of its independence in
relation to things and above all to fellow-men, in spite of all
the enmeshment in a collectivity. In this sense, everyone is
a "one," though an uncompleted "one." If we consider this
particular essential characteristic of human being, it is revealed to us that it is perhaps necessary to "think against"
the *logos* that always already leads and determines us in
its shape of a received way of thinking and speaking. For
when we speak of the one, we always immediately think it
as a one that stands in opposition to the many and the
other. What is meant primarily is always a one that is
closed off and complete, be it in traditional logic as it was
already inaugurated in Western thought with Parmenides,
particularly Plato's Parmenides, and continued through
Hegel's determinations of the relation of the One and the
Many in the *Science of Logic*, as well as in the colloquial
sense connected with the word "one." Because we do not
want to abandon "oneness" as a particular characteristic,
we shall add to the "one," in the description of life experiencing meaning, a hyphen and *-many*. This hyphen is intended to express that, in our life experiencing meaning, we
always find ourselves "in the company of" the "many," despite the fact that we are a "one." This uncompleted, open
"one" does not belong in the element of the cogitative mind
but in the facticity of life.

Only if we approach life experiencing meaning from
the outset as such an uncompleted "one" can it be seen
that, on the basis of our facticity, it is possible for us to
project and integrate contexts of order within the relation
of coexisting contexts of meaning.

Through this process of integration, the contexts of
meaning take on a different meaning in each respective
case. There is, however, a fundamental question: is the life
that *experiences* meaning not also a life that *endows* mean-

ing, as it was the case for Husserl insofar as *the* world as a whole was the construction of on the part of life endowing meaning in the form of an "absolute subject." Perhaps Husserl only asked this question with regard to the endowment of meaning because he was still caught in the tradition, which sought ultimate foundations. Even if the ultimate origin he looked for was certainly no longer the metaphysical "ultimate ground," the movement of his thinking still bears the traits of a speculative constructing that seeks to grasp something at work "behind" the phenomena of experience. In contrast, if one restricts oneself to what we are capable of finding, any quest for an ultimate meaning-endowing instance is excluded from the outset. Only this can be said: in its integrational project, the life that experiences meaning, thought as the uncompleted "one" (one-many), interprets the contexts of meaning from its own perspective. This interpretation is able to change an already existing meaning of different contexts in one aspect or another. This holds to a low degree for certain contexts of meaning, like those founded by technology. Thus, we change only very little to the meaning of the context of traffic as one within which we move. The situation is different in the case of the world of dreams, in which our imagination continually brings about changes. Only the truly great artists, statesmen, and philosophers may be called "creative" because they are able to consciously "institute" the meaning of an epoch in art or the history of thought. Ordinarily, however, we are carried along in the contexts of meaning into which we are born; they are "self-evident" to us. We have received them in learning our language and we cannot withdraw from their "meaning in itself." But this "in itself" should not be understood in such a way as if it could do without the life that experiences meaning which, in dwelling among meanings, understands them, interprets them, and articulates them. It cannot be determined unequivocally whether meaning is endowed by the respective life experiencing meaning or by the contexts of meaning into which it is born, and which language always mediates for it anew. Apparently, the role in this endowing of meaning as far as can be discerned from the phenomenon, is distributed in different ways, according to the context of meaning at issue, in which the life that experiences meaning moves.

II

If we succeeded in thinking the facticity we have expounded, in a philosophical determination, and to "get a grip" on it through understanding, perhaps this would afford the possibility of a transformation of the human "relation to the world." Instead of hankering after the one, "hale" world in fruitless longing, instead of suffering the "alienation" and "fragmentation" of the relation to the world, man could regard the fact that he can and must be in many contexts of meaning simultaneously as a great *gift*. This would be the case precisely because in our time the peoples of the world have moved closer together and are dependent on each other, and precisely because, in the face of the terror of the atomic bomb, the development of the consciousness of this "giftedness" into a human attitude, into a *"hexis"* would be what is "timely." The possibility on the part of human beings of moving simultaneously in many contexts of meaning, when developed into an attitude of character, could even become the trait of "magnanimity" understood appropriately, which no longer ascribes priority to one or a few subworlds in a one-sided manner. Magnanimity can develop itself further; it can lead to the insight that each people has the same right to its particular character as any other in every respect. It can even develop into a "kind" attitude with regard to fellow-men. The insight that the unclosed "one" (one-many) is in its essence always already "in the company of" contexts of meaning also entails, of course, that one is always "in the company of" one's fellow-men. Indeed there is no context of meaning which does not already include the meaning of fellow-man. One only has to think of living on a street in a town or of the way in which we are always already together with others among the institutions of our town or our country; one can think of the world of our profession, of the world of communities, of the cultural worlds in all their contexts of meaning. Above all one can think, as we have already mentioned, of the political world of our time, which is becoming increasingly comprehensive. There is no solipsistic world; world always bears in its essence the character of our fellow-man.

Thus, if the human "one," through the constitution of its being, is always already "in the company of" these social contexts of meaning, this means that this "one" itself, in its essence, is "communalized." Kind is that individual who no longer understands himself as a principally "closed-off" one and who, therefore no longer apprehends his fellow-men as "alien" others to whom he first had to establish a connection, to whom he would first have to "cross over." He has rather gained insight into his own basic constitution as an unclosed "one" and thus, now, as a "communalized" one. The "kind" one knows that he is never among "alien" others, but rather always in the company of the other who is near to him. The essence of our fellow-man consists of being able to be a nearest "neighbor" because the unclosed, communalized "one" is "near" to the other through the structure of "being-with." The experience of this nearness is not the result of a Utopian design, but rather the expression of the fundamental constitution of man. Because of the fact that everyone is, essentially, near to the other, there is also the possibility of reciprocal acknowledgment on all sides, which does not require any kind of "crossing over" from one side to the other. Yet this kind person also knows that although he is always already "in the company of" his fellow-men as his neighbors, in accordance with his basic constitution as an unclosed "one," he nevertheless does not lose his "independence" because of this. He knows that essence lies in being "in the company of" his fellow-men without losing his character of selfhood, without losing his self as that which is peculiar to him alone, just as the other does not have to give up his unique character in being in the company of the first person. It is precisely this phenomenon—that each individual is a one in the sense of a wholly irreplaceable being, although he is always already "in the company of" his fellow-men—that constitutes the greatest and the most astonishing expression of the "richness of Being." It should be the most powerful occasion for philosophical amazement that "everyone who bears a human face" has an individually different face, that no two persons have the same character while yet being aware that he is always already "in the company of" the others. It is precisely in this that the human realm differs from all others. This fundamental heterogeneity of human communal being can only be grasped through the thought of a twofold way of Being that appertains to man alone: man is a "one" which is not closed-off with respect to the others and is nevertheless able to retain what is unique in him. Kind acknowledgment means precisely this: being mutually or universally "in the company of" one's fellow-men in such a way that this being-with does not disturb the peculiarity of one's fellow-man but, on the contrary, attempts to encourage him precisely in his own uniqueness.

It has already been mentioned that the life that experiences meaning develops hierarchies within the relationship of coexistence on the part of the many contexts of meaning and that it "integrates" them. But is there a criterion by which one could judge if these hierarchies are "good" or "bad," or even "evil"? To the basic characteristics of the relation among the contexts of meaning, belong those of free transition, flexibility, and openness. These are the basic characteristics that guarantee an area of free play for the life that experiences meaning, within which it is able to realize integration. This possibility of developing hierarchies within the already existing contexts of meaning—or, in rare cases, by means of the creation of new contexts of meaning—is what we call human *freedom,* which is thus a freedom within the limits of human facticity by which we *have to* be in many contexts of meaning simultaneously, though not necessarily in this one rather than that one.

This freedom provides a criterion. For the essence of what is worse or even evil with regard to what is good, is also made up by the fact that it either hampers this freedom or even makes it wholly impossible. A hierarchic order of contexts of meaning in which *one* leading context of meaning subordinates all others in such a way that the free possibility of movement, and thus the essential "being-with" of the unclosed "one" (one-many), is hampered or destroyed, is in this respect a bad or even an evil hierarchy of contexts. Thus, in totalitarian states, a hierarchy is imposed forcibly in which the context of meaning of the state has absolute priority over all other contexts, in particular those of work or family life and of cultural activity; by this, the life that experiences meaning is no longer able to move freely and to integrate within the many contexts of meaning, in which it can thus no longer avail freely itself of its basic possibility of being-with. Thus, evil is revealed here only insofar as it restricts or even destroys this relation of coexistence of a plurality of contexts of meaning, that is, free transition, flexibility, and openness. Conversely, a hierarchy of contexts of meaning is revealed as "good" when these basic characteristics can come into play freely, and when, in addition, they are unfolded through the particular order to attain greater creative vivacity and are transformed in the attunement which runs through order as a whole. This is the case, for example, in the project of a hierarchy that is oriented towards a religious context of meaning. The attunement of the sacred is communicated to all other contexts of meaning. Similarly, the leading context of meaning of art attunes all other contexts of meaning in such a way that even the sober contexts of utility gain a joyous and more active attunement and are transformed correspondingly.

But how do matters stand in the case of the ethical? For we justifiedly expect from the ethical in particular that, as something "good," it will allow an area of free play to as many contexts of meaning as possible. As we saw in the previous essay, the ethical, like religious and artistic life, is also not a world beside all the many other worlds but rather an active force that permeates all the individual worlds. As a force permeating everything it imparts itself to all contexts of meaning and elevates them by coloring them through and through.

We have to ask, finally, in how far the ethical force of the capacity for com-passion sets contexts of meaning and worlds free in such a manner that they can retain their independence and uniqueness to the greatest possible extent? We have seen that the one who has been transformed in the element of attunement and of intuitively rational "seeing" and "hearing" can encounter his fellow-men and the social communities in which he lives as someone feeling sympathy, and that he can find the right way to comport himself towards them in each individual case. This has only been made possible by the fact that the transformation has seized his whole being. His whole being: this means that his whole life experiencing meaning and comporting himself, not only towards his fellow-man and his community, but also towards things and the world, has become different. How is this to be understood?

We called the healing force at work in the one who is torn out of his everyday indifference a force that determines the whole character of this person. For the purpose of our investigation, we made an abstract distinction within this force with regard to the relation to the other on the one hand and to the community on the other hand, because the relation to one's neighbor and the relation to sociality itself are two phenomena that cannot be traced back to one another. When this transformation by the healing force has established itself in both regards in an individual and, when his *ethos* has developed into the virtues of acknowledgment, compassion, neighborly love, and social sympathy, then this force must also be at work when we relate to contexts of meaning and worlds, for the life that experiences meaning and world belong together. It is unthinkable that humans can live without relating to worlds, without bequeathing contexts of meaning or creating new ones, just as it is unthinkable that contexts of meaning enter into our sphere of experience that are not related to us as intuiting, thinking, bequeathing, or creating human beings.

How can it be shown even more precisely that the one in whom the force of the capacity for com-passion has begun to work is related in a transformed way not only to fellow-men and societies but also to contexts of meaning and worlds? The transformation of someone who is disposed in an indifferent attunement into someone who has "awakened" and who is committed, is marked by the fact that he has for the first time experienced what is other *as* other in the actual sense of the word, as that which he himself is not and never can be. When before, in the attunement of indifference, he was always related to his environment in such a way that he measured and treated what was "other" than himself according to his ideas and wishes, indeed with the continual egoistic tendency to refashion it in correspondence to his will, now, after the experience that has transformed him, the other appears to him for the first time as the one who, as the *other,* has his own interests. Equally, he encounters what is "other" than himself in the form of the totality of the life-world constituted by humans in communal structures. Now he has developed, let us add, an eye for the other contexts of meaning and the worlds in which he used to live as a matter of course before and to the plurality of which he used to be related indifferently, when he did not differentiate them in their individual otherness or treat them accordingly.

Of course, the transforming force does not bring about such an attitude all at once. Also in regard to the many worlds—being no different in this than in the case of the relation to the other individual and to the community—a long path of experience is necessary before the individual has actually developed within himself the transformed mode of encountering alterity.

To summarize, the *ethos* issuing from the capacity for com-passion is a force informing our life that experiences meaning in a particular way. It is the potency active in living accomplishment, which sets free everything that is

other, and in this setting free pervades our life that experiences meaning. At one with this it also pervades the experienced contexts, the worlds themselves; in its aura the
other appears as the other and the many as the many. It is
one and the same light in which the life that experiences
meaning and the world are immersed, and the same light
unites all the contexts of meaning and the worlds experienced in this way. The unifier, that which founds unity, is
itself precisely that which allows each individual context of
meaning, each individual world in the plurality of contexts
of meanings and worlds, to come forth in its own right: the
transformative healing force.

In the one who has been taken out of his everyday attunement of indifference, the capacity for com-passion thus
acts as the all-pervading force that is alive in his overall relation to world, fellow-man, and community. It is the measure that exists here on earth, determining him through
and through in all his contexts of meaning.

Notes

Introduction

1. Werner Marx, *Is There a Measure on Earth?*, trans. by T. Nenon and R. Lilly (Chicago and London: Chicago University Press, 1987).

2. Ibid., p. 51.

3. Ibid., pp. 20–21, 57–60.

4. Ibid., pp. 59, 68.

5. Ibid., pp. 54 ff.

Chapter 1. Is A Non-Metaphysical Ethics Possible?

1. J. Habermas: *Moralbewusstsein und kommunikatives Handeln* (Frankfurt: Suhrkamp, 1983), p. 190.

2. In complex analyses, Käte Hamburger has investigated this indifferent and ambivalent state of having com-passion in her most recent book, *Das Mitleid* (Stuttgart 1985). In the determination of this phenomenon, she proceeded particularly from linguistic usage. One has to note here, however, that in a procedure of this kind the phenomenal analysis can always only show those features that have been given expression in the linguistic usage under consideration. That is to say: starting from the contingent linguistic usage, the full range of characteristics of a phenomenon cannot be revealed in a universally valid way. For this would presuppose that any contingent use of a word would possess a binding force beyond this contingency, which is already not the case because one case of linguistic usage replaces the other.

In addition, all use of language is relative to the human society that uses and "needs" this or that kind of language in order to bring the structure of meaning of its respective life-world to word. Above all, however, we have to bear in mind that, especially in ethical questions, we cannot take a certain form of human communal life as a measure, indeed not even (and particularly not) the way in which man lives first and foremost within any given context of the life-world: in the mode of Being of indifference.

Chapter 3. Ethos and Sociality

1. *Erfahrung und Urteil, Untersuchungen zur Genealogie der Logik* (Hamburg: Felix Meiner, 1954), p. 75.

2. Ibid., p. 24.

3. Ibid., p. 52.

4. Ibid., p. 29.

5. In his *Anerkennung als Prinzip der praktischen Philosophie* (Freiburg: 1971), Ludwig Siep has shown this convincingly. The quote is from p. 145.

6. F. W. J. von Schelling, *Ausgewählte Werke Bd. 7. Schriften von* 1806–1813 (Darmstadt: 1973), p. 303.

Chapter 4. Is There One World?

1. Edmund Husserl, *Die Krisis der europäischen Wissenschaften und die transzendentale Phänomenologie* (Husserliana VI) (The Hague: Martinus Nyhoff, 1954), p. 113; *cf. Edmund Husserl: Erfahlung und Urteib* (Hamburg: Felix Meiner 1954), p. 25 ff. (§ 7).

Chapter 5. The Life-Worlds in their Plurality

1. On the problem of relevance, see Alfred Schütz, *Collected Papers,* vol. 1 (The Hague, 1962) and vol. 2 (1964); *Studies in Phenomenological Philosophy* (The Hague, 1966); *Reflections on the*

Problems of Relevance (New Haven, 1970), *Theory of Relevance* (The Hague, 1978).

The social and pragmatic character of the life-world in connection with "social actions" has its basis for Schütz in "systems of relevance." Appropriating insights originating in Husserl, Schütz shows through phenomenological analyses, among other things, the role of our habitual store of knowledge (acquired among other things through sedimentations of our language); the manner in which types and themes are formed and, within their horizon, the genesis and structure of "provinces of meaning"; and the function of motivations of "in order to . . . " and of projections of social actions.

A conception of the problem of relevance, which differed from Schütz' theory, was developed by Aron Gurwitch. Cf. *The Field of Consciousness* (Pittsburgh, 1966), p. 340 ff and our discussion below.

Index

Absolute, 13; Spirit, 106; subject, 133

Acknowledgment, 48, 55, 57, 62, 63; of others, 66, 67; principle, 77; reciprocal, 135

Action: agreement oriented, 36; in communal world, 47; foundations, 1; guidelines, 2; human, 2; motivation, 107; responsible, 43, 44, 66; social, 143*n1*

Affecticity, 108

After Virtue (MacIntyre), 35

Alienation, 101, 134; from community, 73

Alterity, 128, 130

Analysis: conceptual, 7; critical, 10; phenomenological, 4, 6; secular, 10

Angst, 12, 15

Anteilnahme, 58

Anxiety, 46; universality, 60

Apel, Karl Otto, 36

Aristotle, 5, 15–16, 31, 32, 34, 35, 36, 38, 51, 76

Art, 72, 85, 100, 121, 122, 123

Association, 98

Assumption, metaphysical, 13

Attention, 97, 109, 110, 111, 112, 121; to things themselves, 5

Attention à la vie, 109, 110, 111, 112, 119, 121

Attitudes: changing, 15; character-forming, 61; compassionate, 12, 23; contrary, 34;

disintegration, 50, 52; ethical, 23; fixed, 50; generalizing, 79; prepredicative, 21, 41, 46; set, 52

Attunedness, 15

Attunement, 27, 45, 49, 72, 73, 84, 107; changes in, 34; character of, 46; of commonality, 59; of community, 60; definition, 46; emotional, 12, 15, 16; of forlornness, 50; of horror, 40, 55, 78; of indifference, 50, 51, 52, 53, 54, 58, 62, 73, 78, 90, 92, 93, 94; with insight, 55; mood in, 73; of mortality, 64; prepredicative rationality in, 51

Autonomy, 3

Befindlichkeit, 15, 27, 45

Behavior, changing, 10

Being: and chaos, 78; communal, 136; divine, 43, 64; of entities, 33; experiences in, 44; of indifference, 55; in-the-world, 46; joyful, 46; in life-world, 73; of man, 39, 41, 46, 58; other, 32; outside-oneself, 77; social, 51, 73; structures, 9, 33; truth of, 49; two-fold way, 136; understanding of, 8; with-the-other, 131

Being and Time (Heidegger), 8, 12, 18, 46, 73, 83, 89

145